T0294789

Social Networking and Chinese Indigenous Management

Author: Luo Jar-Der

Translator: Zhou Yong

Polisher: Zheng Chao

Paths International Ltd

社会科学文献出版社
SOCIAL SCIENCES ACADEMIC PRESS (CHINA)

This book is the result of a co-publication agreement between Social Sciences Academic Press (China) and Paths International Ltd (UK).

Social Networking and Chinese Indigenous Management
Author: Luo Jar-Der
Translator: Zhou Yong
Polisher: Zheng Chao

ISBN: 978-1-84464-305-9

Paths International Ltd
Published in the United Kingdom
www.pathsinternational.com

A Chinese Old Saying:

"The Best Leader Is The Leader Who Does Nothing against Nature."

How and Why?

Contents

Preface

This booklet is a compilation of my lecture notes and may serve as an easy-to-understand reading for students and ordinary readers after reorganizing. It is, so to speak, a summary of my research efforts in the management field over the past sixteen years. This book answers the following questions with a sketchy conceptual framework.

When it comes to leadership, why do Chinese always emphasize that the best leader is the leader who does nothing against nature?

When it comes to management, why do we often say that ethical mind is the base for successful business?

When it comes to governance, why do we say that one can govern the whole world if he understands part of *Lunyu* (also known as the *Analects of Confucius*)?

Why do Chinese generally believe that people should seek to be sincere in their thoughts, rectify their hearts, polish their characters and regulate their families before they can order well their states (or they can manage well their organizations)?

Why do Chinese believe that the ideal governance is "myriad things run together without interfering and grow together without harming"?

Why has China always been in a vicious cycle – loosened control leads to prosperity; prosperity brings chaos; chaos results in tightened control; tightened control leads to recession; and recession is followed by a new round of loosened control?

Why is it a common phenomenon in China that one prefers being a leader in a small organization to being led in a big one?

Why is it common in Chinese enterprises that within an organization, there is generally a bureaucracy to control a network of comparatively independent subunits? There are different forms of self-organized units within an enterprise, such as affiliated subsidiaries or self-directed teams, contracted out business units, independent local branches, profit-center departments or internal startup teams.

Why do Chinese enterprises always network with each other to realize an all-win situation? There are regional business groups such as the one of Wenzhou-based enterprises①, small

---

① WenZhou is a county in which most people are businessmen and form various business groups to run business all over the world.

enterprise networks such as the one built on the Yiwu Model[①], platform-based models such as MediaTek[②] providing technology platforms to cottage mobile phones manufacturers and Taobao providing service platforms to online stores, network consolidators such as Li & Fung, and industry networks characterized by one town focusing on a single industry. Outside an organization, there is generally a network of cooperative partners.

The above-mentioned structures –the independent subunits within and networks of cooperative partners outside an organization– are extraordinarily competitive in China. In contrast, large Chinese enterprises that consolidate the whole value chain generally operate inefficiently with exception to labor-intensive "blood and sweat" factories.

Why are there always cliques within Chinese enterprises, together with countermeasures to undo policies from higher levels and, collectively, circumvent bureaucratic management?

How to explain all those common local organizational phenomena in China? I have been carrying out research and teaching for eighteen years, during which I do research mostly by means of participatory observation in enterprises. I ate and lived with entrepreneurs. I have also served as a consultant for some enterprises and been engaged in organizing e-commerce companies and non-profit organizations. All those experiences urge me to think about the above-mentioned local organizational phenomena.

It all started with a surprise in 1996. A Japanese student who studied his doctoral degree in U.K. wanted to research high-tech industry clusters and invited me for cooperation. With assistance from an industry magnate, I obtained an opportunity for entering this field and started researching the governance of outsourcing-service in China's high-tech manufacturing industry with my student. We visited 44 related enterprises before making in-depth field study on two world-leading high-tech products manufacturers, one in Dong Guan, Guangdong Province, and the other in Suzhou, Jiangsu Province. Our researchers usually spent three to nine months observing operations in their factories. Also, before gathering information on the general network within a company, I tended to require the researchers to carry out observation in the company so as to make necessary localized modifications to the questionnaire introduced from the west. That is how I have gradually accumulated qualitative and quantitative management research information over the past eighteen years.

It is through the above-mentioned qualitative research that I have seen a multitude of differences between organizational behavior and managerial practices of Chinese and what is written in the management textbooks coming from the Western managerial research results. For

---

[①] YiWu is also a county in which many small factories generally run their own small stores so as to form a large network of value-chains.

[②] MediaTek is a Taiwanese firm providing IC technology solutions for all kinds of cheap mobile phones.

example, A managerial practice derived from the Western social-network research results always encourages companies to conduct job rotations, because rotations promote more interrelations, establish bridges between departments, and increase communication channels. Human-resource (HR) management practices also advocate job rotations, because they add challenges and fun while diversifying employees' job skills. Nonetheless, such managerial practices are questioned by the owners of some medium-sized Chinese enterprises. They dare only to conduct job rotations within a limited scope while preventing employees, in a planned manner, from familiarizing themselves with all the departments lest they open similar companies and compete with former employers after mastering all the technical details and customer relationships. In a worse possible scenario, a group of employees rather than a single one resign so that the company suddenly loses a large number of excellent employees, who then all become its competitors.

How to solve such managerial problems? And what are the causes? We often say that Chinese prefer being a leader in a small organization to being led in a big one. Such a national character has obviously been baffling SME owners. Moreover, since Chinese like joining a small group or clique, it is not uncommon that a group of persons rather than a single one resign and start their own business. How to explain this phenomenon? How to solve these managerial problems facing by business owners?

I used to study statistical methods and quantitative models, which are doubtlessly common and mainstream methods in the field of management. But such methods are built on established grand theories. After seeing that so many local managerial phenomena in China cannot be well explained using Western managerial theories, I could do nothing but return to management field study by making interviews, participatory observations, organizing focus groups and carrying out grounded theory data analysis. It is through qualitative research and participation in an organization's business operations that I have been working to find out an indigenous theoretical direction.

An explanatory framework based on indigenous social sciences and psychology has come to my mind. I believe that all the phenomena discussed above are essentially rooted in "favor-exchange society" or "guanxi society" ("guanxi" is the Chinese term for social relations. In its narrow definition, guanxi means only familiar ties. The third chapter will discuss this concept in detail). Chinese workers all know the importance of relationship contexture or, in Chinese, Ren Mai (a Chinese term indicating a focal person's ego-centered social network in which social capital is embedded; in the following, I will use the term "egocentric guanxi network" to indicate this concept). They focus, when at work, on enhancing their relationship contexture, because their future achievements at work will largely dependent on its depth and breadth. The enhancement of the relationship contexture relies on favor exchanges at usual times, and many of the familiar ties created during such exchanges are the very resources available for realizing personal achievement and goals. It is through favor exchanges that Chinese realize their respective dreams. Knowing that it is impossible to build success on personal heroism, Chinese turn to rely on the power of a group of people and know that they should share the resulting profits with these people. It is therefore easy for a group of people to form a small group or "guanxi circle" (a Chinese term indicating a group of people bonded together tightly in order to struggle for resources collectively. Chinese often call it "small circle" or "circle", too. The fifth chapter will discuss this concept in detail) in which they share both profits and losses. The best way to capitalize on the Chinese phenomenon of guanxi circles is to let them self-organize into teams so as to achieve all-win situations in particular fields. Otherwise, guanxi circles in a bureaucratic organization will unavoidably evolve into cliques or, in Chinese, Pai-Xi (a closed clique which often struggles for its self-benefits and hurts the interest of the larger network, just like what organized crime does to the whole society), which fight each other, develop countermeasures to undo policies from higher levels and follow tacit rules, which are, in general, those unspoken norms leading to unethical behaviors.

Self-organization process and self-organized units are the keys to explaining the Chinese organizational behavior. They lead to organizational networks that ally with each other or act as downstream or upstream to each other. That is why Chinese organizations are always mainly in a network structure. Pay sufficient attention to self-organization process, make good use of it, and learn to manage self-organized units– all these are the very things that Chinese managerial wisdom is rooted in.

In addition to having taught organization sociology and relevant courses for teen years, I began teaching management including organizational behavior, relationship management and entrepreneurship in 1997. Gradually, I include my research results into these courses by talking about the characteristics of Chinese leadership – the best leader is the leader who does nothing against nature; differentiated mode of association in Chinese guanxi; kind, authoritative and ethical leadership; as well as dynamic balance in managerial processes; talking about favor exchanges, the phenomenon of guanxi circles, and network-like structure of Chinese organizations in management classes. This set of courses is growing mature thanks to discussions with EMBA students and post-graduates, as well as my own experiences from practices and as a consultant. On one hand, I am preparing for publishing a book by incorporating my past research results into this explanatory framework. On the other hand, I recorded and compiled lectures that I presented for a course that I taught at Xi'an Jiaotong University in 2009. This collection of lectures is easier to understand than academic writings and it is translated into this book. Since this book is only a collection of my lectures, I try to make it easier for general readers and will not use too may academic terms and the format of academic articles.

Since this book is not a precise academic writing, I did not emphasize the logic of the argumentation. Instead, I focused on presenting my research results in a language that is easiest to understand. Since it is not an academic writing, this book will be published in the form of compiled lectures instead of an academic paper. But some necessary citations of academic papers are still included in.

In addition, this book differs from popular readings that I write for students from businesses and popular readers. Specifically, this booklet is more scholarly and refers to a lot of theories, so it can still be used as a textbook for universities. It is somewhat like a popular science book. I hope that this book can guide undergraduates, postgraduates and popular readers who have an interest in theoretical knowledge into the field of Chinese indigenous management, and help them to understand how social sciences look at the management in Chinese culture.

Last but not least, please allow me to express my gratitude to My Ph.D adviser Mark Granovetter, who instructs my readings on the articles related to this study, even in today, 20 years after my graduation from Ph.D program. I also feel appreciate for Professor Meng-Yu Cheng of Feng Chia University. I used in my lectures some cases that I had studied together with him. And my gratitude also goes to Shi Xiaolin, an editor at the Social Sciences Academic Press (China), and the Chinese-to-English translator. It is very difficult to translate speeches, not to mention so many Chinese terms and concepts. But they have done an excellent job to greatly increase the readability of this book.

Luo Jar-Der

At home in Tsinghua University, 2010

Lecture 1 Dynamic Balance – The Origin of Chinese Management Thoughts

Phenomena such as preferring being a leader in a small organization to being led in a big one, being inclined to form a guanxi circle, join in a clique, etc., indicate that Chinese are good at self-organizing by means of egocentric guanxi networks.

A Chinese enterprise is generally a small bureaucracy to control a large network of self-organized subunits, enterprises organized into regional business groups, networks of strategic alliances, outsourcing services and industrial center-satellite systems – all these show that Chinese organizations are generally in a network-like structure.

"Ethical mind is the base for a successful business," "one can govern the whole world if he understands only part of *Lunyu*," etc., all these Chinese old sayings suggest that guanxi management is essential for good governing of self-organized units in a network-like structure.

I believe that self-organization[①], the network-like structure and guanxi management are the main keys to understanding the nature of Chinese management. And they can all be traced to Zhongyong, or the doctrine of dynamic balance, developed by Ziji, the grandson of Confucius, more than two thousand years ago.

I believe that the doctrine of dynamic balance (the original translation is "Doctrine of the Mean", but I think that "mean" is not precise) educates managers to improve themselves in three aspects – delegation of power, sincerity and dynamic balance.

1.1 The Doctrine of Dynamic Balance

The book *Zhongyong*, or the *Doctrine of Dynamic Balance*, starts by saying that "What Heaven confers is called the 'nature', Accordance with this nature is called the 'Tao'[②], Cultivating oneself by Tao is called the 'education'". What is called "nature" is principle, which is from Heaven. Obeying the principles of Heaven is the Way, which is the very thought embodied in "The Way models itself on nature." The *Doctrine of Dynamic Balance* then says that "When joy,

---

[①] Self-organization indicates an automatic process making a disordered system become ordered. In this book, self-organization is used to indicate a mode of governance structure. This will be detailed in Chapter 6.

[②] Tao is a concept coming from Taoism. It can be simply defined as the ultra-truth of the universal.

anger, sorrow and pleasure have not yet arisen, it is called 'the state of equilibrium', When they arise to their appropriate levels, it is called 'harmony'. 'The state of equilibrium' is the great root of all-under-heaven. 'Harmony' is the penetration of the Way through all-under-heaven. When equilibrium and harmony are actualized, Heaven and Earth are in their proper positions, and the myriad things are nourished." A person is unbiased when he has no emotions and desires. This is called equilibrium, or the root of the Way. When a person's emotions arise but have not departed from the principle of Heaven, it is called harmony. The effects of the Way are to maximize both equilibrium and harmony, so that all under Heaven are where they are intended to be and keep growing.

The aforementioned set of ideas translates into behaviorism leadership in governance. In other words, it is a set of ideas that focus on little control or not to interfere in people's lives. Just as the *Doctrine of Dynamic Balance* says in the end that "in The *Book of Songs*[①] it is said: 'He makes no show of his moral worth, yet all the princes follow in his steps.' Hence the moral man by living a life of simple truth and earnestness alone can help to bring peace and order in the world. In The *Book of Songs* it is said: 'I will keep in mind the fine moral qualities which make no great noise or show.' Confucius remarked, 'Among the means for the regeneration of mankind, those made with noise and show, are of the least importance.' … 'The workings of almighty God have neither sound nor smell. There is nothing higher than that.'" Therefore, the doctrine of dynamic balance claims that, the best leader never makes frequent appearances or big noises or shows, and even never makes sounds or sends out smells. Such ideas restrict the top-down expansion of powers and, instead, encourage people to organize, grow up and coordinate on their own so that they are satisfied with their positions and, as a whole, keep growing. It is also believed that such self-organization will lead to good order in society.

With regard to contemporary management, the principle of "The Doctrine of Dynamic Balance" asserts that power should come in a bottom-up rather than top-down manner. As a result, an organization that was naturally developed is self-organized, rather than a top-down regulation system, and an organizational structure that was naturally developed is a network-like structure, rather than a bureaucracy. In this case, the grass roots will self-organize into autonomous groups, which in turn will interconnect into a network. In such an organization dominated by self-organization processes, the most effective incentive would no longer be higher pays, better benefits or dividends, but instead would be opportunities to self-organize – people are fully authorized so that they may decide what to do and how to do it, realizing self-organization and self-governance.

The Chinese are a nation good at self-organization. Here self-organization is defined as a

---

[①] This is one of the main six books edditted by Confucius. It is also translated as the Book of Poetry.

governance model based on expressive relationships, common identity, shared vision and trust, as opposed to hierarchy (or hetero-organization), which is built on top-down powers, or to market, which is based on transaction relationships, self-interest, free choice and free competition. Since the Chinese society is built on favor exchanges and guanxi, naturally formed organizations based on guanxi are extraordinarily well developed. "Si-She" (literally, non-governmental voluntary association) formed beyond blood relationship already existed as early as in the Western Han Dynasty. Professor Meng Xianshi discovered, when researching the phenomenon of association in Dunhuang region in the Tang Dynasty, that association was on a voluntary basis, as village residents could join in voluntarily, not necessarily all the villagers having to join in. There were democratic discussions and decision making, well-organized management system and "She-Tiao", or an agreed-upon code of conduct for the members.

That is why the deliberate fragmentation of the economy is always so popular in China – the private sector is full of startups, SMEs, outsourcing service networks, business groups and regional industry clusters; and within an organization, there are always contractors, businesses that reach an agreement with the organization to operate in its name, independent subsidiaries, sub-groups, self-directed teams, internal start-ups, etc. And according to Chinese managerial wisdom, the best leader is one who knows delegating powers to others and, thereby, maximizes their vitality and creativity.

Thus, it is advisable to know how to make good use of self-organization when Chinese carry out management. First-class leaders know how to best use personages, especially those who are able to operate particular businesses, those who can make great achievements even when they work thousands of miles away from the headquarters. Second-class leaders do well in using talents, to form solid teams to realize business wins, one after another. Good managers are experts at making use of relevant regulations, business processes and instruction systems so as to organize the human resources; they can create an organization as disciplined as an army. Unfortunately, however, there are many leaders who, once achieving a little success or grasping a little power, would begin favoring sycophants to satisfy their own needs for complacency. When it comes to Chinese management, therefore, the first question would be: Are you good at using personages? If you are, then you know well about the essence of Chinese management. If you do well in organizing talents into a team, then you are a good leader; if you know how to organize people into an enterprise, then you are a good manager. What if you can do no more than using scum while blowing your own trumpet (there are quite many leaders, of course, who are unaware that they are actually having sycophants work for them. Instead, with blandishments from these lackeys, they think that these guys are once-in-a-century talents)? Let self-organization be and use it to stimulate the creativity and vitality of personages' and talents'– these constitute the origin of a piece of Chinese wisdom, i.e., "The best leader is the leader who does nothing against nature." As for managerial wisdom under the doctrine of dynamic balance, the very first idea is just self-organization.

For the part of Chinese, loosened control tends to bring prosperity. Loosened control allows space for people to self-organize and, thus, is the greatest incentive for Chinese. With this stimulus at work, Chinese are able to show their highest efficiency, creativity and vitality. On the other side of the coin, however, is that prosperity often brings chaos. How can we, then, loosen control without causing chaos? Sincerity is the answer, according to the doctrine of dynamic balance.

Sincerity covers three things. The first is guanxi management, or to manage nine types of guanxi required for governing the state and the world under the doctrine of dynamic balance. The second is ethical leadership, or to set oneself as an example and to educate all the people through one's following a high ethical standard. The third is values- and vision-oriented leadership, or to be extremely sincere to all.

1.2 Guanxi-Orientated Management

According to the Tao of *Doctrine of Dynamic Balance*, nine things should be done to govern the world, "… All who have the government of the kingdom with its states and families have nine standard rules to follow; the cultivation of their own characters; the honoring of men of virtue and talents; affection towards their relatives; respect towards the great ministers; kind and considerate treatment of the whole body of officers; dealing with the mass of the people as children; encouraging the resort of all classes of artisans; indulgent treatment of men from a distance; and the kindly cherishing of the princes of the states.." The first ones concern how to run a government, but, instead of being about organizational hierarchy, orders, rules and workflow designs, they are about how to deal with different types of people. The remaining ones are not about how to govern an organization, instead they recommend how to govern the people – the governor should be kind and placating the people so that they can live and work in peace and contentment. Therefore, guanxi management is valued in the doctrine of dynamic balance; and we can loosen control without causing chaos only when various social relations are managed well.

On the other hand, the top one among the nine things listed above is cultivating one's own character. In other words, guanxi management is rooted in behaving one's self. The *Doctrine of Dynamic Balance* says that "Do not do to others what you don't want done to yourself." "In the way of the superior man there are four things, to not one of which have I as yet attained[①].-To serve my father, as I would require my son to serve me: to this I have not attained; to serve my prince as I would require my minister to serve me: to this I have not attained; to serve my elder brother as I would require my younger brother to serve me: to this I have not attained; to set the example in behaving to a friend, as I would require him to behave to me: to this I have not attained." This is the very meaning of "set oneself as an example", which is at the core of ethical leadership discussed in the field of indigenous management in China. It is not easy, of course, to practice all these, just as Confucius said that he had been unable to fully practice any of them. Aren't there Chinese sayings that "Plant what you want to harvest" and "It is better to teach by what you do than by what you say"? The leader should always do what he wants the organizational culture to be like. Otherwise, all the slogans, tenets and instructions, however many there may be, would become useless, for the leader would lose the others' trust sooner or later, even if he can fool them for some time.

Cultivating one's own character is rooted in sincerity, and that's why the *Doctrine of Dynamic Balance* says that "It is only he who is possessed of the most complete sincerity that can exist under heaven, who can give its full development to his nature. Able to give its full development to his own nature, he can do the same to the nature of other men. Able to give its full development to the nature of other men, he can give their full development to the natures of all creatures and things. Able to give their full development to the natures of all creatures and things, he can assist the transforming and nourishing powers of Heaven and Earth. Able to assist the transforming and nourishing powers of Heaven and Earth, he may with Heaven and Earth form a tripod (for supporting the whole state)." In other words, with utmost sincerity, leader can let all the people live in harmony and, ultimately, let all things be in their proper positions and keep growing.

From the perspective of contemporary management, an entrepreneur can win the trust of excellent talents only when he deals with them sincerely. To start with, the entrepreneur should ask himself: "Are you serious doing this? Will you spend all your time and energy exploiting the business opportunity that you have found? Or are you only one of those who follow suit in a startup bubble, or even a guy who works out a business plan only to swindle investors for a try?" If he himself doesn't believe in this business opportunity and is not really willing to devote time and energy to exploiting it, the entrepreneur will doubtlessly fail to let others feel his passion. And a manager should always first ask himself: "Do you really believe you have an excellent business model? Can you set yourself as an example in creating a corporate culture that you are advocating? What exactly is the corporate vision you are promoting, a real life-long belief or

---

[①] Confucius admits that these behaviors are even too hard to be achieved for himself.

only a corporate announcement?"

In addition, both institutional designs and governance mechanisms are of course important for the purpose of loosening control without causing chaos. According to Chinese managerial wisdom, however, only institutions are not enough, as the sincerity of the leader is indispensable. Personal sincerity of a leader will move others and turn into the organizational culture and vision. There is a Chinese saying that "If your ways are different, you cannot make plans together." In other words, people can group and succeed together only when they have the same dreams and ways of doing things. The Tao of an individual can be popularized among and attract many others and, thus, become the Tao shared by a group of people.

As a result, first-class leaders treat excellent people with sincerity; good managers know how to gain their subordinates' loyalty using benefits and regulate their behavior using rules; and incompetent managers know no more than coercing their subordinates by power. Unfortunately, there are now so many managers who would put on airs even if they have only a little power. Daring not delegate power to others, they want to do nothing but grant approval and maintain control. They think, wrongly of course, that all the other people will live in fear of their authority and be lured by the promise of gain. From the viewpoint of real talents, they are nothing but puppets.

Only with sincerity can the leader propose a vision for the organization, move the employees so that they would follow him, and realize values-oriented leadership. The very first idea from managerial wisdom under the doctrine of dynamic balance is guanxi management, which is rooted in sincerity.

And very similar ideas are also seen in the book The Great Learning, which says that "The ancients, who wished to illustrate illustrious virtue throughout the world, first ordered well their own states. Wishing to order well their states, they first regulated their families. Wishing to regulate their families, they first cultivated themselves. Wishing to cultivate themselves, they first purified their minds. Wishing to purify their minds, they first sought to be sincere in their thoughts. Wishing to be sincere in their thoughts, they first extended to the utmost their knowledge. Such extension of knowledge lay in the investigation of things. Things being investigated, knowledge became complete. Their knowledge being complete, their thoughts were sincere. Their thoughts being sincere, their minds were then purified. Their minds being purified, their characters were cultivated. Their characters being cultivated, their families were regulated. Their families being regulated, their states were rightly governed. Their states being rightly governed, the whole world was made tranquil and happy." It also says "From the emperor down to the ordinary people, all must consider cultivating their characters as the root of life. It cannot be, when the root is neglected, that what should spring from it will be well ordered."

The investigation of things, extension of knowledge, sincerity of thoughts and rectification of minds – these constitute the base for the cultivation of the self, only after which is it possible to regulate one's family, govern well one's state and realize a peaceful world. *The Great Learning* also points out that governing a group of people, from a family up to the whole world, should always be based on the cultivation of the self, which in turn is based on the sincerity of wills and correction of minds. This perfectly matches the ideas from the *Doctrine of Dynamic Balance*.

1.3 Dynamically Balance Yin and Yang

With regard to the doctrine of dynamic balance, what impresses us most is probably not the above-mentioned utmost sincerity, managing guanxi and educating all the people through one's following a high ethical standard. Instead, it is the idea that one should adhere to the doctrine of dynamic balance principle. This is from the book "*Shang Shu·Councils of the Great Yu*": "human hearts are unfathomable, nature of Tao is subtle. The only way to achieve the nature of Tao is to focus on nothing but the pursuit of dynamic balance." According to the *Doctrine of Dynamic Balance*, "Confucius said: "There was Great Shun[①]:-He indeed was greatly wise! Shun loved to question others, and to study their words, though they might be shallow. He concealed what was bad in them and displayed what was good. He snatched up the two extremes, determined the Mean, and employed it in his government of the people. It was by this that he was Great Shun!"

"Snatched up the two extremes and facilitated their balanced nature" means that, first of all, Chinese always regard all things as an integrated system. Secondly, Chinese can always tolerate any two opposite forces, and let them coexist within an integrated system – Yin and Yang are compatible with, rather than repelling, each other, despite their being of opposite natures. As an ultimate result, equilibrium is reached between the two opposite forces, instead of imbalance caused by either of them overpowering the other. And this is the very core idea embodied in the Chinese Taoism, or the Yin and Yang Symbol, as follows:

[①] An ancient great Chinese emperor.

The Yin and Yang Symbol is about not only the coexistence of two opposite forces within a single system, but more importantly, dynamic changes in the system. In other words, the complementation and competition of Yin and Yang offset and convert into each other, before ultimately reaching equilibrium. Equilibrium leads to in-equilibrium and the next run of balancing process, so it is a dynamic process of balancing Yin and Yang. In the meantime, the system is able to continuously renew itself and, hence, to keep growing. The so called system can be an organization or an enterprise; it can also be a regional economy or even the whole society or country.

According to the *Great Learning*, "On the bathing tub of T'ang[①], the following words were engraved: "If you can one day renovate yourself, do so from day to day. Yea, let there be daily renovation." In the Announcement to K'ang, it is said, "To stir up the new people." The *Book of Odes* says, "Although Chau[②] was an old state the ordinance which lighted on it was new." In other words, the *Great Leraning* sees all things in the world are in constant change, and a system is therefore impossible to stay still; otherwise it would be lifeless. According to the theory of the *Great Learning,* systems renew themselves on a daily basis; and Chinese are in pursuit of the renewal of themselves and the mandate being sustained anew, that is, they try to vary with changes in the situation from time to time. In such a constantly changing system, "dynamic balance" is not to be "the mean" between black and white, or between left and right. Instead, it allows the coexistence of black and white and of left and right in a system by balancing them. That is what is meant by "The myriad things grow up together without harming each other, and they follow their courses simultaneously without interfering with each other."

Zhongyong means dynamic balance. Moreover, it is about keeping dynamic balance in a constantly changing system so that Yin and Yang coexist and are compatible with each other. As a result, neither of them is too strong to cause the loss of diversity, of the vitality from interactions among disparate parts and of the capacity of self-correction within the system.

Since Zhongyong means keeping dynamic balance in a constantly changing system, "love to question others, and to study their words, concealed what was bad in them and displayed what was good (like the Great Shun did)" becomes very important. And it is even more important to know how to rebalance a system after learning the cause. Just as the *Great Learning* says, "The point where to rest being known, the object of pursuit is then determined; and, that being determined, a calmness may be attained to. To that calmness there will succeed a tranquil repose. In that repose there may be careful deliberation, and that deliberation will be followed by the attainment of the desired end." Determination, calm, tranquility, deliberation and attainment –

---

① An ancient Chinese emperor, who was taken by Confucius as one of the best Chinese leaders.
② A Chinese dynasty, from BC. 1046 to BC. 256.

Start from determination and you can ultimately make the right decision, find a new direction and rebalance the system.

What is, then, to be dynamically balanced?

"The best leader is the leader who does nothing against nature" reveals how to lead a self-organized system, in which dynamic balance is the method to control a threshold over which the system transits from one phase to another. This concerns two extremes in the system—too much coupling at one end and too much decoupling at the other. If good governance is unavailable, then, at the end of too much decoupling, everyone is atomized, self-organization is impossible and, in the resulting chaos, everybody competes with all the others; and at the other end, too-much coupling leads to a closed network that is united internally and aggressive externally – fragmentation or even dogfight will occur in a larger network. If good governance is available, then the bottom-up power enables a group of people to self-organize into an orderly social network and to develop a code of conduct. Such a network enables self-governance and will not lead to cliques which hurt others' interests. Good governance stays somewhere between insufficient and excessive self-organization.

Another aspect of dynamic balance concerns how the leader conducts bureaucratic management. If he fails to manage things well, then there are two possible consequences. On one end, everything is left uncontrolled and, hence, thrown into chaos. On the other end, excessive controls make bottom-up self-organization process impossible, and thus devitalize the system. In contrast, a good leader always knows when to grant powers to others so as to avoid excessive control, and when to tighten control by certain management policies.

Management under the *Doctrine of Dynamic Balance*, therefore, pursues proper, top-down hierarchy control, on one hand, and proper, bottom-up self-organization, on the other. These two things tend to interact and compete with each other. Therefore, dynamic balance has a third aspect – the balance between hierarchy-relevant powers and self-organization-relevant ones.

Last but not least, the *Doctrine of Dynamic Balance* aims to realize management such that "The myriad things grow up together without harming each other, and they follow their courses simultaneously without interfering with each other." In other words, it aims to let a diversity of things coexist, complement and compete with each other, operate in harmony, and keep growing. Only through delegation of power is it likely to realize self-organization, diversity and prosperity. Only through showing sincerity to all and educating all the people through one's following a high ethical standard, a leader may make various things to coexist in harmony, naturally grow in prosperity and to work for each other. And only through dynamic balance is it likely to avoid excessive control over this dynamic, open and complex system, on the one hand, that makes diversity disappear (a unified system is lifeless). On the other hand, dynamic balance will avoid overly loosened control; that results in disorderliness and collapse of the system. It was after reading Confucian classics that Akio Morita, the late co-founder of Sony, realized the meaning of Confucianism in corporate management is: let everything growing naturally and sustainably.

How, then, can we realize the balance discussed above? "The best leader is the leader who does nothing against nature" means anything but letting things be. On the contrary, we should do many things before we are allowed to do nothing. This requires the leader to first become perfectly sincere and keep working till all the people are fully educated by his sincerity, according to the *Doctrine of Dynamic Balance*. Only by the time that all the people reach a certain level of morality, will they start self-organization and self-management so that the world is well governed even if the leader does nothing against nature.

Lecture 2 The Essence of Chinese Management

2.1 China's Management Philosophy

There has been a set of management philosophies in China since the ancient times. Some scholars prefer talking about them on the basis of the *Yi Jing*, also known as the *Classic of Changes*, while I prefer doing this on the basis of *Doctrine of Dynamic Balance*. The *Yi Jing* and the *Doctrine of Dynamic Balance* are, of course, from the same origin – the traditional Chinese way of thinking.

Chinese thinking is primarily characterized by the belief that nothing is isolated from the others. Instead, they view all things as parts of a complex system – the Yin and Yang Symbol is a typical example of this systematic thinking. This system has a very important characteristic – Yin and Yang always coexist instead of either one existing alone. In the Yin and Yang Symbol, for example, there is a white dot on the black side and a black one on the white side; instead of mixing into gray, black and white always coexist no matter how they change relative to each other. A system would die if there was only one color or voice in it. A system would lose the impetus for evolution if it had no elements that complement and, compete with, each other. It is harmony despite disagreement, plus the coexistence of various elements, that is advocated in Chinese society. Continuous growth is possible only when all the elements correlate and interact with each other.

We can gain a correct understanding of "Zhongyong", or "dynamic balance", only after we understand the Chinese systematic way of thinking. Dynamic balance is the best state advocated by Chinese. Nevertheless, it is much more than simply splitting the difference. The term "Zhongyong" was translated by the west into the Doctrine of the Mean as a result of absolute misunderstanding. Zhongyong is not the statistical mean or a middle state that is neither black nor white (or neither bad nor good). Such a middle state – being gray rather than black or white, being in the middle rather than on the left or right, or all the people neither agreeing nor objecting to something – results in embarrassing mediocreness. A system in that state is lifeless. "Zhongyong", in its real sense, should be translated into the Doctrine of Dynamic Balance. Like what is shown by the Yin and Yang Symbol, Zhongyong means a dynamic process where black and white coexist and change relative to each other for ever. The core idea of the doctrine of dynamic balance, therefore, is the inclusion of differences into a whole. Specifically, you adhere to your principles while allowing others to follow theirs so that both diverse voices and interactions are maintained in complementary and competitive relations. Zhongyong aims to always keep dynamic balance among all the elements, and that is the very meaning of "All things keep growing."

If we look, on the basis of the systems theory contained in the *Doctrine of Dynamic Balance*, at the organizations defined in the Chinese way of thinking, we may then draw the following conclusions:

Firstly, an organization is an orderly, open and complex system.

Secondly, this system is built upon multiple elements; there are always a lot of self-organized units within the organization; and that "The best leader is the leader who does nothing against nature" is the highest management standard.

Thirdly, instead of being dominated by a particular element, the organization consists of multiple elements that coexist and complement and counterbalance each other.

Fourthly, a good system is characterized by differences creating connections and vice versa. Generally speaking, differences result in disconnections while connections lead to similarities. That is in contrast with a system created under the doctrine of dynamic balance – the bigger the differences, the closer the connections; and close connections will not make the differences disappear.

In other words, different elements within an organization interconnect with each other, and such connections lead to communication and resource flow among these elements. It is this type of communication that brings creativity and innovation and, hence, system changes and development. This system will not be full of similarities and ultimately become the same everywhere because of difference but connections. Otherwise, it would be dead. And this system will not become disconnected because of differences. Otherwise, it would collapse into separate parts and, hence, result in lack of order.

Last but not least, what Chinese management philosophies deal with is the very structure of complex network systems described above, and organizations are therefore able to keep growing with continuous innovation and development.

Reflecting the essence of Chinese management as presented in the *Doctrine of Dynamic Balance*, research efforts by local sociologists represented by Professor Fei Xiaotong (Fei, 1992) have also reached very similar conclusions, mainly including:

(1) Egocentric guanxi networks in the differential modes of association: This is the very origin of Chinese self-organization, which is characterized by being guanxi-oriented and expanding with family ethics at the core;

(2) Order under the rule of rituals: Informal regulations play a major role while formal laws play a minor one; laws and rituals work together; and attention are paid to both laws and

interpersonal relations in the pursuit of lawsuit-free society;

(3) The best leader is the leader who does nothing against nature: Self-organization is valued. The fact that the emperor's power has no effect on the countryside means that the emperor knows how to restrain his power such that self-governance by clans is made possible;

(4) Ruling by elders: Education is more often used than is tyrannous power and is prioritized over punishment so as to realize kind, authoritative and ethical leadership;

(5) Balancing between the emperor's and the gentry's powers: Coordination and balancing between the top-down, hierarchy-relevant powers and the bottom-up, self-organization-relevant ones are required to well manage the interactions between them.

These five qualities of Chinese society mentioned by Mr. Fei Xiaotong happen to match the five pieces of managerial enlightenment from the *Doctrine of Dynamic Balance* as follows:

2.2 The Essence of Chinese Management

2.2.1 Guanxi Management

We will come to realize that guanxi management is the key to good governance of self-organized units. Guanxi management is also covered by the *Doctrine of Dynamic Balance*. "… in the handling of the realm, a state or a clan, there are nine basic patterns of treatment …" actually suggests that the leader should properly manage his relationships with the ministers, vassals, ordinary people, etc. Also, for the purpose of good guanxi management, the *Doctrine of Dynamic Balance* discusses four ways to prevent us from doing to others what we don't want done to ourselves. This is obviously a characteristic of ethical leadership, as the leader is required to educate all the people through his following a high ethical standard.

Guanxi management is an important part of Chinese management, but what exactly is it? There is no strict academic definition. This term is apt to remind us of bad things in manipulating guanxi (in Chinese term, la guanxi), such as giving bribes or making a deal through the back door by utilizing personal relations. The guanxi management I'd like to discuss herein has, indeed, nothing to do with manipulating guanxi. In reality, actions aimed at short-term gains, such as manipulating guanxi, are harmful to good guanxi management.

Specifically, guanxi management mainly covers two things. On the one hand, there are always numerous types of guanxi in an ego-centered network, such as those of internal followers, of independent teams and of external organizations (e.g., partners and outsourcing service providers). How to establish long-term relationships with these relations such that both sides can cooperate for a long period of time and ultimately realize an all-win situation? This is an issue that guanxi management needs to address. On the other hand, since there is generally, within a Chinese organization, a bureaucracy to control a network of comparatively independent subunits and, outside the organization, a network of cooperative partners, there is a corresponding interface between the formal bureaucracy/institutions/rules and the informal guanxi/networks. How to deal with this interface? What things should be decided in accordance with these institutions and what others should be handled through these networks? How to identify these two types of things so that an organization can operate in a flexible and orderly, rather than disorderly, manner when it is under loosened control? All these issues fall into the scope of guanxi management.

Good guanxi management creates an atmosphere of harmony and trust among all the parties such that various activities can operate smoothly, rapidly and inexpensively. And such phenomena as the so-called "manipulating guanxi" and "making a deal through the back door" result from the misuse of guanxi and networks. The prevalence of these malefactions within an organization demonstrates the leader's failure in guanxi management.

We will expatiate on these issues in Lecture 3, Guanxi Management, and Lecture 4, Dynamic changes of Guanxi.

2.2.2 Become Perfectly Sincere to Build Guanxi Circles

Situation determinism developed by Chinese indigenous anthropologist Francis L. K. Hsu in his book "Clan, Caste and Club" (1963) suggests that Chinese building personal guanxi circles is a cultural habit that they are unable to change. Such circles, however, can become vicious by turning into closed cliques, or places where there are countermeasures to undo policies from higher levels and where tacit rules are followed. Fortunately, you may also make them positive – turn them into powerful incentives through "enfeoffment" (i.e., let them self-organize into self-directed teams and develop themselves in particular fields).

The management mode highlighted in the *Doctrine of Dynamic Balance* is not hierarchy-based control, but vision- and values-oriented leadership. The primary task of management is, therefore, to become perfectly sincere, according to this Chinese classic. Everything starts from sincerity. It is necessary for the leader to make him a good example for others and to create values and vision for the organization. Only by so doing can he set a common goal for the subordinates, who can then well manage themselves. And this will culminate in harmony based on dynamic balance, avoiding the scenario where all the people work for different goals.

"Able to assist the transforming and nourishing powers of Heaven and Earth" is the very goal of the above-mentioned management philosophies. Briefly, we should work to let all things keep growing. Instead of making the organization big and strong and competing for short-term gains, we should build it upon a solid basis so as to realize sustainable growth.

With the enfeoffment-based mode of team building, a Chinese organization tends to be structured such that there is, within the organization, a bureaucracy to control a network of comparatively independent subunits and, outside the organization, a network of cooperative partners. At the top of the organization, there is still a complete set of institutions, regulations and processes, with the emphasis placed on working in accordance with them. Nonetheless, there are a lot of networks, such as internal teams built around the key leaders, semi-independent business units that are contracted out and, outside the organization, networks of outsourcing service providers and strategic alliances. Institutions and regulations within a Chinese organization are therefore not stiff, but flexible enough to allow for the functioning of internal and external networks. Smart leaders are those who know how to leverage the human capital. Instead of restricting the employees with stiff regulations, they know how to use networks to achieve successes no matter where they are. This will grant the employees sufficient power and freedom to develop in particular fields, on the one hand, and assure that they will remain loyal, on the other. For this purpose, there should, of course, be a set of governance mechanisms that center on trust plus institutions. Trust comes from guanxi management, which in turn starts from one's becoming sincere, cultivating oneself and setting a good example for others. In China, therefore, governance is carried out under rituals and laws together.

All these will be detailed in Lecture 5, The Guanxi Circle Theory – Motivation of Chinese to Work.

2.2.3 Self-organization

The Chinese managerial wisdom described in the *Doctrine of Dynamic Balance*, is first of all manifested by paying much attention to self-organization; and the last managerial idea discussed in this class is just "The best leader is the leader who does nothing against nature." We may emphasize, therefore, that self-organization is the primary reason why Chinese organizations are so efficient: you are given opportunities for being "enfeoffed" and establishing a "family" that consists of a group of persons with whom you are familiar and have guanxi contracts. In other words, you have a field where you develop, make efforts and share results with the members of your own guanxi circle. This indeed is the primary source of the overall efficiency of a Chinese organization. Do-nothing leadership is wisdom, confidence in others and the daring to grant powers, and it will lead to network-like organizational structures. In Chinese cultural context, it is where the most efficient organizations will ultimately appear.

Since it objects to the possibility of any single, dominant power preventing the other powers from functioning, the *Doctrine of Dynamic Balance* says that "In terms of transforming people, sounds and appearances don't amount to much … In the functions of Supreme Heaven, there are no sounds or smells. It is 'perfect.'" It is meant to say that using forceful means is the last way to manage people. Real good management does not always come with top-down control. Instead, it is carried out with "no sounds or smells" to let people manage themselves and, naturally and spontaneously, create order. Such do-nothing-against-nature leadership is, of course, only what Chinese dream about ideal society, and has never been fully realized.

The concept of self-organization as a type of governance structures was not first developed in China, nor was it developed by sociologists. When they talk about self-organized unit in society, sociologists often use the term "community". And when they talk about self-organization in enterprises, management scholars often use such a term as "network". Nonetheless, self-organization is the very thing at the core of organizational phenomena and managerial behavior in China. There are always different kinds of independent units within a Chinese organization, such as independent subunits that operate in the name of this organization, business units that are contracted out, self-directed teams and internal startup teams. And outside the organization, there are regional groups of businesses, outsourcing service networks, clusters of small businesses and towns that each focuses on a single industry. Why then is it like this?

The common phenomenon of self-organization actually derives from a traditional Chinese thought. Chinese generally prefer being a leader in a small organization to being led in a big one. To secure opportunities for self-organization, Chinese are willing to work hard: They may join other people's circles, work to the latter ones' advantage, but at the same time, build up their own interpersonal relationships and wish to form their own teams someday, etc. A smart leader will take advantage of such a working motivation, knows when to recognize the employees' right for being the leader of an independent team in a particular field, and make it be the strongest incentive for them to work. In contrast, a leader who does not understand this always attempts to control everything and refuses to give the employees opportunities for self-organization. Under his leadership, therefore, guanxi circles will ultimately evolve into cliques, along with infighting, countermeasures against policies from higher levels, and even attempts to displace him.

Such a Chinese thought results in a common phenomenon – there are usually energetic, independent, small teams within Chinese organizations. There are connections inside and inter small teams to emerge into a network structure Self-organization and the network structure are the very things that let Chinese enterprises have advantages such as flexibility and rapid response to environment changes.

This concept will be detailed in Lecture 6, Self-organization as a Mode of Governance.

2.2.4 Governance under Rituals and Laws together

We can see that good process of self-organization relies heavily on governance under rituals and laws together. Governance under rituals comes from what we refer to as guanxi management. Specifically, it is advisable for the leader to create a trustable environment, conduct ethical leadership and make himself a good example for others so as to establish the organizational culture. And governance under rituals also comes from the leader's becoming perfectly sincere. In other words, the leader should define a vision and direction out of sincerity, and this is the only way to realize governance under rituals. On the other hand, governance under laws constitutes the foundation for equity and the ultimate guarantee for compliant behavior. In the meantime, self-organization can be well governed only when rituals and laws work together. "Advocate rituals and respect laws", as proposed by Xun Zi (a Chinese Confucian philosopher who lived during the Warring States Period), is the greatest piece of wisdom from the traditional Chinese culture.

Governance under rituals and law together is characterized by the coexistence of formal and informal institutions. It is not that Chinese society does not respect laws, but only that it also emphasizes that there are justification and affection in addition to law. Chinese society is most afraid of stiff laws. In other words, all the people would be deprived of motivation and vitality if there were stiff laws for everything with no flexibility at all. That was why the Qin Dynasty, which upheld ruling under stiff laws, was subverted fifteen years after it was founded. All the post-Qin dynasties learned lessons from it and allowed certain flexibility outside their formal institutions. For this purpose, governance was also carried out under rituals. What was referred to as "rituals" in ancient China was actually a set of informal institutions. Both organizations and the overall society could develop continuously and steadily only when governance was carried out under rituals and laws together. Otherwise, there would be a time of turbulence or ossification.

The current mainstream managerial philosophies have often left enterprises and the overall society in ossification in the Chinese cultural context, which I refer to as "a vicious circle of modern management." With regard to the management of large organizations and the overall society, there being a lot of regulations left unenforced is the very problem. If we take tight control as the only means of management according to the hypothesis of rational man , when so many people in the organization have countermeasures against policies from higher levels, more regulations will be developed and supervision strengthened till they are finally followed by nobody. In other words, everybody work under tacit rules with no respect for regulations or laws, which instead become an instrument for rent seeking and finding fault.

All the smart leaders, therefore, know that they should define simple regulations but enforce them seriously. Unfortunately, a more common phenomenon at present is that there are stringent regulations but that they are poorly enforced and, ultimately, obeyed by nobody in today' China.

Accordingly, the Doctrine of Dynamic Balance, when it comes to management, aims not to create a big machine that perfectly executes every order of higher levels, but to realize the scenario where "The myriad things grow up together without harming each other, and they follow their courses simultaneously without interfering with each other." In other words, diverse things coexist, complement, compete with and stimulate each other. And this is the only way for creativity and vitality to stay and for the dream of sustainable growth to come true.

And I will explain how to realize governance under rituals and laws together in Lecture 8, Dynamic Balancing between Governance under Rituals and under Laws.

2.2.5 Dynamic Balance

The ways of the Great Shun are always valued in China. The *Doctrine of Dynamic Balance* says that "-He indeed was greatly wise! Shun loved to question others, and to study their words, though they might be shallow. He concealed what was bad in them and displayed what was good. He snatched up the two extremes, determined the Mean, and employed it in his government of the people. It was by this that he was Great Shun." It means that order in a society ruled under rituals is built upon the leader's virtue and influence, before various forces can be dynamically balanced and a harmonious and stable society established.

The above-mentioned statement emphasizes that we are able to continually adjust our behavior to the ever-changing contexts in a dynamic environment. With regard to self-organization versus bureaucracy, trust versus power, and governance under rituals versus that under laws, we should always know that neither overdoing nor underdoing is good. In other words, we should never go to extremes or overcorrect; we should return to the right path once we find ourselves deviating from it and, during such continual correction, maintain dynamic balance. China's Yin and Yang Symbol is essentially explaining that Yin and Yang contain, and change relative to, each other, thereby maintaining dynamic balance.

During such dynamic balance, the most important thing is to balance the loosening and tightening of control, or self-organization and hierarchy. I will employ the theories of Elinor Ostrom, Oliver Williamson and Mark Granovetter to explain that the primary balance is established in certain contexts. We will see that self-organization, hierarchy, and market are the three basic modes of governance. Self-organization is suitable for some contexts, hierarchy-based governance for some others and the market for still others. But the doctrine of dynamic balance tells us that every kind of governance contains all the three of them, only that it sometimes leans toward self-organization, some other times toward hierarchy, and still other times toward the market. In other words, they are ideal types, and every governance structure in reality combines these three basic modes. On the one hand, we always, in different structures of governance, seek balance depending upon the context. On the other, each basic mode of governance is inclined to expand itself such that the system gradually becomes unbalanced. And the *Doctrine of Dynamic Balance* instruct us to rebalance it.

With the emergence of knowledge and service economies, self-organization-based governance becomes fit for a growing number of transactions. And Chinese managerial wisdom is the one for self-organization-based governance, as it focuses on educating people, rather than building up business processes. First of all, the leader should judge a person, get him mentally ready for work, train him, and assign him a suitable job, before granting the decision power to him in a particular field and, ultimately, giving an incentive to him through "enfeoffment." All these are done for educating people. What is business? It is transactions. Accordingly, Chinese managerial wisdom, the Chinese way of doing business and governance over transactions are essentially about governing the guanxi contracts with people. Such people-oriented governance over transactions is, as we have emphasized, based upon the common vision, trust, affection, kindness and rituals. Nonetheless, regulations are also critical, because business is business even if you are dealing with your family members. It is always advisable to define rules before you make a deal with someone else. Only with regulations in place can you build an institutional framework and facilitate the establishing of mutual trust. And all these should start from sincerity and the cultivation of oneself. That is why Chinese often say that "Ethical mind is the base for successful business." Such a governance mode as this indeed constitutes the core idea of Chinese management.

Since dynamic balance is at the core of Zhongyong, we will explore it in a number of lectures. Among them, Lecture 4 expounds the instrumental and expressive motives in relations as well as the dynamic balance between trust and power. Lecture 5 is about the dynamic balance between affections and equity inside and outside guanxi circles. Lecture 7, as we have discussed above, explores the dynamic balance between formal and informal institutions within an organization. And Lecture 8 expounds the dynamic balance between hierarchy-based and self-organization-based governance within an organization.

In the subsequent lectures, I will first of all explain the nature of Chinese society as observed by local sociologists, before finding the most similar western theories to clarify Chinese managerial ideas. In the end, I will present some cases used in the research on indigenous management so as to explain these phenomena.

Lecture 3 Guanxi Management

"... All who have the government of the kingdom with its states and families have nine standard rules to follow; the cultivation of their own characters; the honoring of men of virtue and talents; affection towards their relatives; respect towards the great ministers; kind and considerate treatment of the whole body of officers; dealing with the mass of the people as children; encouraging the resort of all classes of artisans; indulgent treatment of men from a distance; and the kindly cherishing of the princes of the states.."

—the Doctrine of Dynamic Balance

3.1 Explanations from Local Sociologists

Self-organization-based governance relies on an atmosphere of trust, which in turn relies on good guanxi management. There is always a misunderstanding that guanxi management is all about manipulating guanxi for short-term interests. It is indeed opposite to reality, as manipulating guanxi is very harmful to long-term trust and, hence, is the misconducted behavior that should not be done in guanxi management.

Granovetter pointed out that minimal trust exists in all the three basic models of governance. Guanxi management is therefore needed for governance based on either the market, or hierarchy or self-organization. Notwithstanding, guanxi management is the most important in case of self-organization based governance, because the behavioral logic of self-organization is mutual benefit and mutual trust, and the entire atmosphere is consultation for consensus. Chinese society is the one for which self-organization is most suitable, because Chinese are good at guanxi management and, naturally, are apt to build an atmosphere for the governance of this sort. And all these derive from their family ethics.

What is the particularity of relationships among Chinese? In other words, what is the difference between Chinese guanxi and social relations or social ties in the Western society? Fei put forward the concept of "The differential modes of association". He observed that people in the West were bundled into groups like stacks of firewood and that races, occupations, religions, etc., were the criteria for telling them apart and bundling similar ones together; people in the same group were more similar to, and accordingly identified with, each other, and obey the same rules. He referred to such society as "society with a group-based structure."

But that differs greatly from Chinese society.

In Chinese society, social network is like ripples caused by a stone thrown into water, that center on an ego. And the relationships between you, the focal person, and others are just like these ripples. Those who are closer to you have stronger relationships with you. Likewise, those who are not that close to you have weaker relationships with you till you do not know each other – you are strangers with no interrelationship at all. Chinese norms and ethics are actually not unified or universal. Instead, different ethical standards are employed depending upon closeness or interrelationships. Theft, for example, is a bad thing, and you should call the police once you see someone is stealing something. But what if the stealer is from your family? Confucius said that "The father conceals the wrongs of his son, and the son conceals the wrongs of his father. This is fairness!" It means that lying is a bad thing but that it is tolerable if you tell a lie for one of your family members in order to conceal his/her wrong. As the relationships go weaker, requirements from family ethics become less stringent. In other words, the standards defined in family ethics become more applicable for closer relationships.

Next, I would like to explain characteristics of relationships among Chinese with an indigenous psychological theory. The theory of "social-oriented psychology", by Yang Guoshu (Yang, 1993), groups relationships among Chinese guanxi into three categories by closeness: Family ties, familiar ties and acquaintance ties.

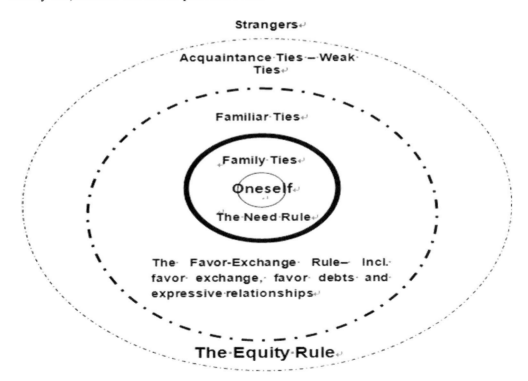

Figure 3.1 The Diagram of Three Types of Chinese Guanxi

Different relationships are followed by different behaviors and ways of addressing conflicts, which in turn cause different results. Taiwanese scholar Hwang, Kwang-Kuo (Hwang, 1987; 1988) also grouped relationships into three types: Expressive, instrumental and mixed ties. These two methods of categorization are essentially very similar to each other, according to Yang Yiyin, a researcher at the Chinese Academy of Social Sciences (CASS). Accordingly, I will then explain them together:

Firstly, family ties, including real and pseudo-family ties. Sometimes I prefer the concept of pseudo-family ties, which also include the closest ties from marriages, adoption and blood brothers (or sworn sisters). The need rule is applicable for such ties. In other words, I should have what you have; you should satisfy, unconditionally, all my needs; and we are not allowed to say anything like "This is mine, not yours", not to mention pricing or bargaining. If a man asks his brother to drive the former's wife to the airport, for example, the latter should not ask the former to pay for it, but do it unconditionally. There should be such a relationship among family members that "I will give you a hand whenever you need it" in China. Briefly, we may say that it is a type of collectivism.

Secondly, the equity rule applies to acquaintance ties, or instrumental ties in Hwang's classification, that is, pricing and bargaining are allowed and fair deals can be made. In this situation, Chinese become perfect economic men. A main quality of Chinese, however, is that there is an important type of mixed relationships between family and acquaintance ties, that is, familiar ties.

Thirdly, familiar ties, i.e., mixed ties in Hwang's definition, are applied for Renqing rule—i.e. the favor rule or the favor-exchange rule. They are a type of exchange relationships under the camouflage of family ties. There are expressive interactions between friends, and the reason we say familiar ties are under the camouflage of family ties is that they will, actually and ultimately, lead to fair exchanges. That is in contrast with family ties where you may take something whenever you need it without having to do anything in return. Nonetheless, although familiar ties will ultimately lead to fair exchanges, such exchanges cannot be made undisguised. Instead, they must be made under the camouflage of expressive ties. Jack did Tom a great favor, for example. Tom was very grateful to Jack and repeatedly said things like "It's just like you saved my life" and "I really don't know what to do in return." And Jack would say things like "It's a piece of cake", "You are my friend and I'd like to do anything for you" and "It's what I should do." But Tom knew that he would need to do something in return sooner or later. This is so-called a "favor debt."

Every Chinese has a number of favor debts in mind. Favor debts have several characteristics. Firstly, it is impossible to square them up. Secondly, they are highly need-specific in the mutual-benefit context – particular services are provided to meet the needs of the other party. Thirdly, neither bargaining nor pricing is allowed, and you cannot make it clear that you are doing this in return. Fourthly, favor debts cover almost all things, such as money, power, knowledge, honor, reputation and emotional support. Favor debts, indeed, are guanxi contracts that don't have to be in a written form and that cannot make it clear what is exchanged for, not to mention the validity period (the longer, the better, of course). But both parties know what their respective rights and obligations are, and neither of them would destroy the tacit understanding.

Although favor debts seem so unclear, each party to them has a roughly clear understanding that what he has received and what he should do in return. This of course needs a common value assessment standard so as to make fair favor exchanges. Otherwise, such ties would break sooner or later if either party has spent much time and energy on the favor exchange while the other party thinks it is just a piece of cake. That is because the former would feel that he has been hurt or even betrayed.

In the Chinese language context, the term "guanxi" generally means all these three types of social ties. But sometime, we may use this term in its narrow-sense definition indicating only strong ties, i.e. including only family and familiar ties.

Which is followed by Chinese, collectivism or individualism? This question is controversial. It is generally believed in the West that Chinese follow collectivism, and quite a many scholars and experts agree on this belief even though they know little or even nothing about this issue. Nonetheless, we often say that the Chinese nation is the most selfish one in the world. What exactly, then, are Chinese like, altruistic or selfish? Liang Qichao (a most-prominent scholar, journalist, philosopher and reformist during the Qing Dynasty) launched a debate about whether Chinese were like pieces of sand or a single piece of clay. Sun Yat-sen (the founding father of the Republics of China) believed that Chinese were just like pieces of sand; Lu Xun (a famous novelist in the early 20 century) also believed that Chinese were the most selfish people in the world, as represented by Ah Q, the protagonist in the *True Story of Ah Q* written by Lu Xun. But I think that the answer is not that simple.

The behavior of Chinese, indeed, is changeable. In the case of family ties, including real- and pseudo-family ties, Chinese are collectivistic and are willing to be altruistic to their family. In the other cases, however, they become increasingly individualistic. As Francis L. K. Hsu put it, the behavior of Chinese is characterized by situation determinism. In one situation, you are in my circle and he outside it. In another situation, however, you become an outsider when another person closer to me appears. To sum up, Chinese deal with people in their circles in a way different from the one when they deal with outsiders, that is, their behavior changes with the situation.

3.2 The Relevant Theories in the West

You may often see a Chinese show off and say: "I have a big Ren Mai" or "I build up my Ren Mai strategically", etc… What is Ren Mai?

Ren Mai can be defined as an ego-centered social network composed by trust relations. It can be directly translated into relational context, and there is a parallel concept in sociology, i.e. micro-level social capital (Lin, 2001). In other words, it is a set of ego-centered social relations which can bring resources to the focal person. In the following, I will call it egocentric guanxi network.

Why is it called "network composed by trust relations"? Granovetter (1985) argued in an article titled *Economic Action and Social Structure: The Problem of Embeddedness* that trust was the very mediate variable between resource exchange and social ties, and that the level of trust determines how resources are exchanged. Since relationships in China are full of social exchanges, trust plays a critical role in them. Without trust, there is no resource exchange in guanxi. That is why I can define Ren Mai as an ego-centered social   network composed by trust relations.

What then is trust? This is a very big question that deserves much time to discuss. Briefly, trust can be categorized into trust in the broad sense and that in the narrow sense. What Granovetter talked about is the latter, which is called real trust, while what people usually employ is the former. Real trust is based on interpersonal relations, social network structure, identity and common vision, rather than power relations, institutions, general morality, and deterrence methods, such as hostage.

With regard to trust in the broad sense, your actions are predictable for me, so I know what you will do next. I as a teacher, for example, ask my assistant to get some tea for me, and he/she will always do a good job as I expect. That is because I hold the power in the school. Such a relationship is not built upon real trust since there is no risk, according to Granovetter. Williamson (1995) referred to such a relationship as "calculative trust" or it can be called "deterrence trust" (Shapiro, Sheppard and Cheraskin, 1992). And this is the concept of trust used in the game theory. In other words, one party is sure that the game has not ended and that, to secure greater benefits in the subsequent rounds of the game, the other party will behave in a more cooperative manner. In the example mentioned above, the gaming relationship between the assistant and I comes to an end as soon as he or she graduates from the school. By this time, he/she will not necessarily get some tea for me if I fail to leave any influence. When it comes to cooperation between states in the ancient times, the kings often sent to the other state one of their princes as a hostage to signify that "I will not deceive you, because I will suffer a heavy loss if I do." Such a scenario is built not upon real trust, but upon the power over me.

And there is a second scenario – that is, assurance (Yamagishi and Yamagishi, 1994; Yamagishi and Cook, 1998) – on the side of trust in the broad sense. This broad-sense trust is based on network closure and no choice. If I, again for example, want someone to fetch some documents from my office, but only one student knows where the office is, then I would have no choice but to have him do this even though I know that he is clumsy and may be unable to find the documents. This is assurance, also known as committed relation: You opt to believe someone because you have no other choice. This situation occurs in a large number of family businesses. A man in a family-business, for example, may have no confidence in his brother's ability, but he has to, under pressure from the family, let the latter do a particular job. In this case, I can't but trust my brother, since I don't have other choices in the familial closed network. A committed relation bonds two persons together without the possible choice to break up the relationship. And assurance is built upon this committed relation, rather than real trust, according to Granovetter.

Real trust exists only when you make a choice, at certain risks, from among a number of options. I ask the students in the classroom, for example, who is willing to fetch the documents for me. And I select one student immediately after several of them lift their hands. This suggests that I trust him more than others.

Trust can also be categorized into generalized trust and particularistic trust. Specifically, generalized trust refers to trust without particular targets, while particularistic trust targets only specific persons. Simply speaking, with generalized trust, you trust even strangers; and with particularistic trust, you trust only those with whom you have particular relations. Generalized trust is based upon general laws and morality. In other words, people trust a stranger, since his/her behaviors are under the monitoring of laws and morality. When it comes to overall generalized trust, China (including Taiwan and Hong Kong) takes a place almost in the middle of all the measured nations, according to a World Bank survey on the overall macro-level social capital of these nations. Among them, nations in Western and Northern Europe take the highest places. Iraq and some African countries take the lowest places.

Particularistic trust is based upon particular relations. Examples include trust in the narrow sense that Granovetter talked about, or real trust, and what Williamson referred to as "personal trust", neither of which is based upon power or assurance.

In the case of China, trust is based upon things that vary with relationships.

3.3 Guanxi Management: Building an Atmosphere of Trust

3.3.1 From Strangers to Acquaintances: When Trust Begins

Family, familiar and acquaintance ties are indeed interchangeable in the Chinese cultural context, though in ways that vary with times. In the Chinese history, the framework of the guanxi management remains changeless, as favor-exchanges, long-term guanxi-oriented thinking, governance mode of self-organization, and network structure are always important characteristics of Chinese society. Since relationships in the differential modes of association are highly open, however, the ways in which relationships are structured keep changing with times.

Also, relationships among Chinese may change from this ring to another. A typical example is how to turn a stranger into an acquaintance. Chinese have a large number of meals for social purposes, mainly including getting closer to those with whom they already familiar and getting to know new people. Few Chinese would trust strangers, and turning a stranger into an acquaintance is the first step to establish trust.

In China, people get to know strangers with whom they have "nine similarities" (in Chinese, Jiu-Tong), on the one hand, or introducers, on the other. Nine similarities include the following: the same surname, growing up together, being born and growing up in the same hometown, having the same ancestry, getting enrollment into the same school in the same year, being colleagues in the same working unit, being in the same profession and being persons of the same interests. Comparing China with the West, we may see that identification among westerners is mainly built upon some inherent factors that are hard to change, such as gender, geographical region, nation, religion, social status, class, age and race, etc… By comparison, the important identification among Chinese is often based upon non-inherent factors, such as nine similarities—i.e. the same school, profession, working unit, cohort, and interests, in addition to inherent, unchangeable ones such as blood relations and geography. In other words, Chinese tends to create identification based on intimate relations. Categorical thinking is typical of westerners and associative thinking of Chinese, according to Fei Xiaotung's theory and the current studies in the field of cross-cultural cognitive psychology.

Religion, status, age, race, etc., are categorical, while the factors upon which relations among Chinese are built, under the action of associative thinking, ranging from blood relations to kin, geography (people, when away from their hometowns, are usually glad to meet townsmen) and even relations with the same school, profession, working unit and interests. The similar life experience, rather than the same social category, is important for a Chinese to build up guanxi. More people are therefore covered on the basis of family ethics. And that's why there is a

Chinese saying: "Any stranger may be your maternal relative (when you want to build up a new relation)." You can manage to establish ties with someone even if you have no relationship with him at all. Blood relations and geography are of course inherent, and the most effective sources of relationships, but the same life experience in professions, schools, companies, cohorts and interests can also be good reasons to connect.

With regard to the process of establishing ties, I have added the tenth "similarity" to the list of the nine similarities, that is, the common friend of both persons as an introducer. It is often occurred for a Chinese that he or she needs to rely on an introducer to establish ties with others. An introducer actually plays dual roles. Firstly, he may act as the mediator between the two persons in dispute because he is well known to and trusted by both. Secondly, he may act as an assurer. Specifically, if the two persons fail to settle the dispute, then the assurer may have to assure, with his reputation, the aggrieved party of the latter's betray from any loss. And to avoid any damage to his own reputation, the assurer has to indicate that he is not on the latter's side, thereby punishing the latter with the friends' voices.

Why is it so important to get to know strangers by having meals with them? This is because the process of turning a stranger into an acquaintance will change the rules of exchange for both sides. Only after getting to know each other through a common friend as the introducer, will the two persons begin to follow the equity rule. Chinese are, to a great extent, rather distant to real strangers. And "Mind one's own business" is actually the traditional attitude to strangers in Chinese society.

For example, if two vehicles collide with each other in China, for example, both drivers will typically get off their vehicles and have an altercation with each other, or begin to call the police for record and arbitration. But the story would be very different if they find that they are in the same uniform. At this time, they are more likely to say "Forget it" or give reasonable compensation than to have an altercation, simply because they are working at the same organization. In a word, they will generally and ultimately settle the dispute in a friendly manner.

That is the very difference between a stranger and an acquaintance. The equity rule applies when the other party is an acquaintance, but not necessarily does when he or she is a stranger. Instead, there tend to be more doubt and hostility in the latter case. And that is why people in the business world spend much time establishing egocentric guanxi network, or egocentric guanxi network. This indeed is a process of turning strangers into acquaintances.

3.3.2 Building and Maintaining Trust

The "encapsulated-interest account of trust" developed by Russell Hardin (Hardin, 2001) and others explains the process of building trust in acquaintances. The first half of his theory explains this with logic similar to that of the game theory. Firstly, the interacting parties make transactions repeatedly, during which both parties may behave in a trustworthy manner. In this stage, trust may be based on calculation, but is not real trust. With the number of games growing, however (say, the two parties have made twenty transactions), long-term trust can be built since their interests have encapsulated in each other's cooperation. Both parties may gradually develop mental inertia when the other party's behavior is always trustworthy. In other words, they begin to believe that the other party will not deceive them, though this judgment is not sufficiently grounded. It is by this time that real trust begins. Trust in this context is indeed an instrument for reducing transaction costs.

What then is trustworthy behavior? Aneil Mishra (Mishra, 1996) pointed out that one's trust in another is based upon the trustworthiness of both parties, which includes four factors – competence, honesty, consistency and mutual benefit.

Competence refers to that a person should first of all have the ability to do a particular thing so as to avoid the scenario where he or she is unable to finish it though he or she really wants to.

Honesty refers to that either party will not intentionally conceal facts from, or deceive, the other.

Consistency refers to that a persons' attitude and exhibition are continuous and consistent rather than be changeable, inconsistent or different from time to time.

Mutual benevolence is the thing that Chinese care most about. It comprises a lot of elements, of which mutual loyalty is the most important. In reality, Chinese are inclined to overemphasize mutual benefit, as they typically will favor anyone as long as he or she is within their guanxi circles and even to the extent that they think about nothing but his or her concerns about guanxi, with no attention to whether he or she is right or not. Which of the four factors, then, is the most important in guanxi management? There are some primary principles of the trust theory. Firstly, you cannot control others' trust on you and the only thing you can operate is your own trustworthiness. To establish good relationships with others and win their trust, you have no choice but to keep improving yourself till all the four factors listed above become available. There tend to be people who believe that they can win trust simply through some underhand tactics. Unfortunately, however, not all the people are fools, but so many people think they can fool all the others. One may deceive others with his underhand tactics for some time, but his wrongdoing will almost always be detected in the end, because it lacks in trustworthy behavior that is based on fairness, consistency and honesty.

Secondly, trust is built slowly but collapses rapidly. Such is a quality within any network-like structure. Building trust is similar to building a tower in that it is built bit by bit, but collapses suddenly because of several lies or betrayal, like removing bricks from the tower. There will be no obvious change in trust at the first couple of times, but a collapse will occur at the third or fourth time of betrayal.

Lastly, Chinese management always comes with interactions between power and trust, of which the latter is more important than the former. Unfortunately, there are now a large number of managers who overemphasize power and underhand tactics while neglecting a more important thing – the building of trust.

3.3.3 Trust in Family and Familiar ties

Behaving in a trustworthy manner is the best and perhaps the only way of building and maintaining trust with acquaintances. In the case of familiar ties, however, the affective factor is involved because of favor exchanges.

Favor exchanges can be regarded as a form of social exchanges, but it is hard to identify them with the concept of social exchange since they come with the qualities of Chinese behavior. On the one hand, favor exchanges are similar to social exchanges in that one is not allowed to bargain, to ask for immediate reward or even to make it clear. They therefore seem consistent with the need rule, which forbids an asking for reward. Nonetheless, favor exchanges involve deep social exchanges, and we can explain, with the social exchange theory (Blau, 1964), the meaning of trust included in them – both parties must believe in the other party's benevolence and have expectations without asking for immediate reward, so that the game of give and take can last.

On the other hand, favor exchanges have long-term resource exchanges as their core function, so they satisfy the trustworthiness theory. After all, the relationship between two parties will break up sooner or later if one of them fails to show trustworthy behavior, such as failing to record a favor debt into the favor account or to do something in return at the right time, or being never able to do it because of incompetence. Accordingly, the mutual exhibition of trustworthy behavior is another part of the groundwork for building trust under the favor rule.

Notwithstanding, favor exchanges are often about highly exclusive favors, such as: Giving face, i.e., an action making someone feel honored; making face, i.e., an action raising someone's reputation; giving a gift that satisfies someone's interests and that shows friendship, such as a collectible or book that someone has long been desiring; or giving a favor in private, such as helping someone to move or lending him or her a considerable amount of money. That is why favor exchanges are also of an affective nature. Affection will bring an irrational sense of trust, as it may make someone overlook the untrustworthiness in the other one's behavior and, instead, believe that his or her benevolence is real. It is true that favor exchanges between friends are rational, instrumental ones, but daily "affective behavior" will, once and again, strengthen such affective trust.

The story would once again be different in the case of family ties, including real- and pseudo-family ties. A pseudo-family is a small group and, in principle, no member of this group can be neglected, not to mention breaking off ties with him or her. Accordingly and actually, trust in this case is based on both affective and committed relations, so it contains both the so-called assurance and what Granovetter referred to as "real trust." Since family ties are within a very small group, family members watch each other carefully and obey powerful rules of conduct. Accordingly, they must have no other choice, trust each other and, whenever possible, follow the same set of behavioral norms. A man who is chairman of a company, for example, may have to employ his brother and, although the former does not believe in his competence, appoint him to a rather good position however incompetent the latter is. And the latter also must forebear and concede to the former when necessary. A study by Wang Shaoguang, a chair professor in the Department of Government and Public Administration at the Chinese University of Hong Kong, shows that this is why family members are the ones who Chinese most trust.

Toshio Yamagishi and Karen Cook (Yamagishi and Cook, 1998) studied Japanese society and found out that committed relations apply to the broad-sense trust between Japanese. Japan is narrow and small in area and the system of feudal domains (or "han" in Japanese) prevailed in a certain period of time. And the feudal domains were later on superseded by stock companies (or "kabushiki kaisha" in Japanese). Japanese typically work for the same company for life and their behavior is under close monitoring. They will probably be unable to find another job once they are found to have done anything wrong. As a result, Japanese have to appear punctilious, honest and faithful in Japan where they are closely monitored by each other. Once they are outside Japan, however, Japanese typically will begin to become obstreperous. This suggests that the seemingly high trustworthiness of Japanese is actually based upon the committed relations within small circles and that once they are outside those circles, they will not be so trustworthy any longer.

3.4 Dynamic Balancing of Relationships

Behaving in a trustworthy manner requires fairness, consistency, honesty and openness. But the objects in favor exchanges tend to be special, and the more person-specific the special treatment, the better shown the special value of a favor exchange. How to balance fairness/consistency and favor exchanges is a most common dilemma of favor exchanges in the favor-based Chinese society.

3.4.1 Dynamic Balancing between Instrumental and Expressive Motives

Favor exchanges between friends, on the one hand, are actually intended to secure instrumental benefits. On the other, long-term, fair instrumental exchanges will also lead to friendship. Favor exchanges between friends tend to last for a very long period of time. And there are high or even unpredictable uncertainties in this long process. Rational selection and calculation of costs and profits, therefore, will not be very useful and, instead, being compliant will become a very good tactic. On the one hand, the favor giver, under the principle of brotherhood, is not allowed to ask for reward. On the other, the favor receiver, under the principle of reciprocity, is required to remember this favor forever (Luo, 2005; 2011). Both friends, therefore, already have a favor account in their mind and will keep reviewing it. And before either party reaches the limit of his or her tolerance, both parties generally will maintain favor exchanges under these two principles so as to build up their respective social capital for potential needs. This can be called the favor rule in the case of exchanges between friends (Hwang, 1987; 1988). So, an important skill for handling relationships between friends in a guanxi circle is to balance instrumental and expressive motives, as this will maintain trust at a high level. As Granovetter put it, "So individuals have some reason to be continuously scanning relationships to determine the balance of motives [consummatory or instrumental] behind them (Granovetter, forthcoming).

Granovetter[①] speculates that real trust can hardly be built if relationship continues only due to the benefits resulted from the relationship, such as money, prestige, reputation and resources. Rather, it should be based on the consummatory motivation—i.e. relationship continues for its own sake. Your behavior that hurts your beloved person is thus also harmful to you. It is unthinkable for the two sides to betray the relationship of this sort, and real trust can thus be built. As Granovetter puts it (forthcoming, Chapter 3, Page 6):

"So the issue is whether you value a relationship for its own sake, as in love or close friendship, or you value it for something to be gained that is outside the relationship itself. Where your concern about the relationship is not instrumental in this way, but consummatory, then encapsulation of interest is genuine, and any harm to the other's interests, detected or not, would be harmful to you as well.

One the one hand, too much instrumental motives leads to the loss of real trust. On the other hand, pure expressive motives can't facilitate favor exchanges. In the guanxi of this sort, a focal person always need to balance the two extremes— expressive or instrumental motives.

[①] It is cited from Granovetter's forthcoming article "Trust" in the Chapter 3 of book *"Society and Economy"*. I appreciate the special permission of the author to let me cite the book.

3.4.2 Dynamic Balancing between Favor Exchange and Equal Sharing

Chinese indigenous psychologist Zhai Xuewei (Zhai, 2001; 2005), a follower of the situation determinism theory developed by Francis L. K. Hsu (Hsu, 1963), propose some modification to Hwang, Kwang-Kuo's theory. According to the Chinese mental model developed by Zhai, it is difficult to clearly categorize the relations among Chinese, so it is impossible to say which principle applies in which ring; and in reality, different relationship categories constitute a spectrum as indicated by the following figure.

Since there is a spectrum, there are a lot of intermediate colors between which it is less likely to see a clear boundary. We will produce a result as shown in the following figure if we still group the relations into three categories. We can see from the figure that several core concepts constitute the base for Chinese behavior.

The first concept is "society based on family ethics" developed by Liang Shuming (Liang, 1981). This is at the core of morality in Chinese society. That is because a Chinese egocentric guanxi network in the differential mode of association, indeed, expands from family ties in order to include persons, based on the closeness of relationships, into the family. It operates under the need rule, according to Hwang, Kwang-Kuo. Take, again, the man who is chairman of a company, for example. If his brother wants to work at his company, he then has to appoint the former to a position in which there are few jobs to do, however lazy and silly the former is. This is where the need rule works – it is necessary to satisfy, more or less, the needs of one's family. In this spectrum, the color of family ethics becomes lighter as it moves outward.

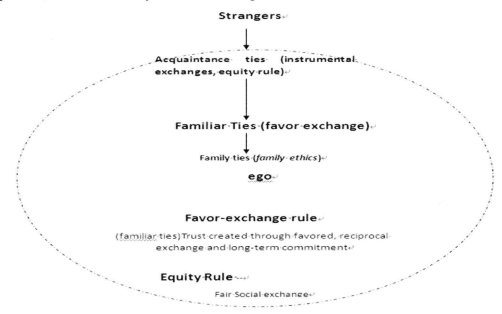

Figure 3.2 Zhai's Model of Equal Sharing and Favor Exchange

By comparison, Zhai believes that even for real family members, the need rule is not really followed, despite the fact that, according to Chinese family ethics, a father should be kind to his children and a man friendly to his younger brothers, who in turn should be respectful to him – this is only the ideal of family ethics. Otherwise, the *Dream of the Red Chamber*, also often known as the *Story of the Stone*, would not exist (this novel depicts the story of a big noble family in the city of Nanjing during the early period of the Qing Dynasty). The maladies and problems with big families, as described by the *Dream of the Red Chamber*, suggest that there are a lot of hidden benefit exchanges even between family members. The principles in family ethics become less applicable as relationships become weaker.

Zhai thinks that the principle in a guanxi circle guiding Chinese behavior is equal sharing. Within the same circle, the primary concern is unequal sharing of benefits rather than only a small amount of benefits being available for sharing. So the most important thing is equal sharing of benefits. Westerners care more about procedural justice – the ultimate shared amount is unimportant, as it is sufficient if the sharing mechanism lets everyone feel the presence of justice. By comparison, Chinese in one guanxi circle care more about distributive justice –the leading member of a guanxi circle should evenly distribute benefits among all the members so that they feel that they have equal access to the benefits. Within a group, a person will feel him or her being pushed aside if he or she receives fewer benefits or even has no access to the shared benefits than do the others. As a result, this person will likely become less loyal to this group. When it comes to the sharing of benefits, there are Chinese sayings such as "Anyone who knows it (i.e., the sharing of benefits) is entitled to a share." They actually refer to "equal sharing" – all the participants should share the benefits. In China, the last thing that a leader should do is refusing to owe success to all the participants and taking all the benefits instead of evenly distributing them among the participants. Accordingly, the leading member of a circle must demonstrate his or her impartiality and selflessness.

Zhai further pointed out that the problem with the need rule that Hwang talked about is its inability to clarify the characteristics of the relationships among Chinese family members. It will lead to a wrong conclusion that a person can always have his or her personal needs satisfied within the family. In reality, the need rule is restrained, within Chinese families, by the distribution mode, as the satisfaction of a member's needs will, under the principle of equal sharing, let the other members feel unfairness. And this will result in the other members' potential need for access to the same amount of benefits. The parents should, at least, hint to the other members at the existence of the benefits. A man is about to marry, for example, and needs a house, and his brother is also single. In this case, it is inadvisable to only satisfy this man's need without thinking about that of his brother. In other words, it is necessary to consider their needs at the same time.

In other words, family ethics asks a Chinese share everything with his/her family members, whose needs are thus more or less satisfied by the focal person. That is why the need rule works in families. For outer rings of a person's guanxi circle, he/she will not share everything, as he/she does in the family, but share "common-pool resources" equally to all circle members. That is, for the guanxi closer to the focal person, the more resources are included for equally sharing. The weaker is the guanxi in one's circle, the less resource is included. Outside one's guanxi circle, the equity rule applies for those pure instrumental exchanges. But when giving benefits to one of his devoted followers, the leading member of a guanxi circle, again for example, must not neglect the other followers and may even need to consider the feelings of people outside the circle of his devoted followers.

In other words, there are no three types of guanxi in Zhai's model; rather guanxi is a spectrum from strangers to family ties. From inside to outside, the force of pure instrumental exchanges increases and the principle of equal sharing decreases.

For example, I once investigated a case when I was in a disaster-stricken area in Sichuan Province. A public charitable organization intended to invest 8,000,000 yuan in a county to construct buildings for the local victims, but the governor of the county said that he was unwilling to launch such projects. That was because this fund was only enough for reconstructing a couple of villages and it was impossible for the governor to identify the ones eligible for sharing it. Villages without access to the fund would begin to complain no matter which villages had been identified. For the purpose of equal sharing and justice, therefore, the governor would rather spend the fund building public infrastructures than distributing it to particular villages or villagers.

Another principle that guides Chinese behavior is that of favor, or the above-mentioned favor exchanges in familiar ties. Unfortunately, the principles of equal sharing and favor often conflict with each other, as the former requires that all the members of a circle be equally treated, including the sharing of resources, while the latter is particularistic, that is, it requires that a particular person in the circle be specially treated. In other words, there are conflicts between particularism and fairness in a larger network.

The leader of an organization, for example, should, throughout the organization, maintain his image as one who upholds equal sharing and justice. In the meantime, however, he must, within the circle of his familiar ties, obey the favor rule, that is, he should favor his followers depending upon the closeness of his relationships with them. If the leader does carry out perfectly equal sharing, there will be discontentment and complaints from his inner circle members: "Given my contribution to you, why do I have to share equally with others?" At this moment, the leader generally will manage to give somewhat larger shares to the members of the circle to show differentiated treatment. But if he/she excessively favors his/her circle members, the leader will cause discontentment throughout the organization.

Conflicts between equal sharing and the favor rule constitute the very reason why Chinese usually work with underhand tactics. Underhand tactics is their only recourse when it is impossible to make trade-offs between the two principles. A better solution is that the leader can give good reasons for favoring his followers and a set of sharing norms acceptable to all. Examples of reasons for larger shares include superior performance at work, personal efforts, good relationships with others, etc. Unfortunately, however, he can do nothing but secretly favor his followers if he can find no good reason. That is when a hotbed for underhand tactics comes into being.

Chinese often need to make trade-offs between the principles of equal sharing and favor. They follow different principles inside and outside their circles, according to Hsu's situation determinism theory. Since they always deal with other persons by determining whether the latter ones are within their circles or not, Chinese cannot follow only the principle of equal sharing or of favor. A successful leader typically lets the members of his circle feel the use of the favor rule, on the one hand, and those outside it, the use of the principle of equal sharing, on the other. Briefly, he realizes perfectly dynamic balance between the two principles.

3.4.3 Dynamic Balancing between Trust and Power

It is actually impossible, for the focal person of a guanxi circle, to always follow only the favor rule. A person who does so is a "good guy", but he will likely become a non-authoritative hypocrite and be faced with disobedient people. Favor exchanges are of course a cornerstone for relationships between friends and trust is critical for guanxi management, but a person who does not know how to exercise power can be anything but a good leader. A real good leader knows when to use power, when to rely on guanxi and how to balance them.

Balancing between power and trust is something commonly seen in enterprises. There is such an example from an outsourcing service provider for a world-class maker of optical disc drives (I had a long-term field study in the factory of this provider). The provider received a big order from the maker. The president was very happy and came back drunk, saying how good relationships he had with the managers of this maker. Nonetheless, he sobered up all of a sudden and, as if he had woken up from a dream, made calls to have employees solicit orders. I felt very strange and asked him why he did this even though he had received this big order. He explained that it indeed was good to receive the big order but that power would become unbalanced since it, alone, represented more than half of the total sales volume at the company. The current sense of friendship would no longer exist once power becomes unbalanced. That is because power and trust interact with each other and the sense of trust will more likely occur if the two parties are equal. And that was why the president must secure other orders as soon as possible in order to reduce the share of this international giant back to 40%. When it comes to personal ties, he had pretty good relations with the maker's president for the Greater China region. When it comes to the production process, the two companies had worked together for years, including joint R&D efforts. But power weighing was always on his mind even if their relations, corporate or private, were already so good. Once severe power imbalance occurred, the party which got the upper hand would no longer pay much attention to the other. This was very clear to both parties.

We can see from this case that Chinese of course value favor exchanges in order to establish long-term, solid exchange relations and also will, in such relations, maintain high trust through the mixture of affective and instrumental exchanges, but that such exchanges are overshadowed by power. In other words, favor exchanges are more likely to occur in the event of equivalent powers; and the party who gets the upper hand, in case of power imbalance, will gradually be inclined to get resources by power instead of favor exchanges.

Of course, Chinese know, even in the event of power imbalance, that they should leave room for favor exchanges. That is because familiar ties will break up soon if either party always oppresses the other by power. Accordingly, another issue for which Chinese always need to realize balance is when to use power and when to leave room for favor exchanges.

3.5 The Levels of Guanxi Management

How these favor exchanges, power and equal sharing are balanced results in different levels of guanxi management.

Speaking of relationships, westerners often have a misunderstanding that they are equivalent to bribes and corruption. In reality, manipulating guanxi for short-term interest is only the lowest level of guanxi management, because this is an action aimed at short-term benefits, often disobeys the principles of honesty, openness, equity and consistency, and damages trust. Moreover, the guanxi manipulator will give lots of resources to whoever is more favorable for him within a short period of time. It is therefore difficult for other persons to expect long-term mutual benevolence and loyalty. In a word, manipulating guanxi is detrimental to the building of long-term trust.

At a higher level, various interests are well satisfied. We often use a Chinese word "Bai-Ping", which means that a focal person exchanges resources among several sides and makes everyone satisfied. Letting all the stakeholders receive benefits seems to meet Chinese expectations for equal sharing; and making a decision on the basis of agreement also meets the expectations for mutual benevolence and loyalty. In the process of "Bai-Ping", however, it is often necessary to tactically promise future benefits, to a party that will likely need to make concessions, in exchange for such concessions. Excessive occurrences of benefiting one party at the sacrifice of another will unavoidably cause impartiality. Moreover, excessive secret promises also will damage honesty and openness. This is a challenging job as it is prone to result in imbalance. And the worst case is the failure to deliver on a promise made to the conceding party, leading to the breakup of ties with him or her.

At a further higher level, favor exchanges are carried out with all the relevant parties. There is a Chinese saying that goes: "Establish as many relationships that enable mutual benefit as possible". It suggests that Chinese hope to extensively establish such long-term familiar ties. In addition, Chinese place extra emphasis on being beneficent and requiting kindnesses; and quick-witted persons will establish long-term ties and trust with those who have not risen in the world. The *Gate of the Lamb*, a novel written by Li Peifu, depicts the story of a capable man (in the following, I will use this term to indicate both capable man and woman) who saved the life of a central government official during China's Great Cultural Revolution and later on, after the official took office again, ran a business with his ties with the official being the most important part of his capital. Such a way of building relationship with others is characterized by one's doing good without expecting reward. It prevents conflicts between short-term equal sharing of resources and favor exchanges, because the latter ones are all on a long-term basis.

At a still further higher level, both parties have common values and objectives and define a win-win strategy. In this case, the building of long-term relationships is based firstly upon common thoughts and secondly upon favor exchanges. It is easier to maintain benevolence and loyalty in a win-win situation. With common values and agreement on how to share benefits, both parties find it easy to adhere to the principles of equity, consistency, honesty and openness.

The highest level for Chinese is that "Great sound is hard to hear. The great form has no shape." Guanxi management at the highest level is not one's operating relationships but relationships being automatically established without the need for him to do anything. It is advisable for a person to be always monomaniacal and trustworthy, adhere to his values and maintain good reputation. He then need not make any efforts to establish relationships with others, as they will be automatically established for him. And he also need not operate egocentric guanxi network, as he naturally will be trusted by many and receive help when needed.

We may say, therefore, that in recent years in China, the biggest misunderstanding about relationships is that manipulating guanxi is everything. And that is why foreigners think that relationships among Chinese are all about corruption and privileges. In reality, manipulating guanxi is something for short-term benefits that some people are forced to do in a hurry because they have failed to do a good job in guanxi management.

Guanxi management, in its real sense, is creating an atmosphere of trust and harmony. This relies on things including: Trustworthy behavior, the building of long-term expressive ties, favor exchanges, the establishment and maintenance of guanxi contracts, adherence to the equity rule in the dilemma of favor exchanges, the establishment of a good code of conduct in circles on the basis of generally accepted moral standards in society, and the creation, in accordance with specific norms, of an environment for public-opinion-oriented supervision in circles.

Unfortunately, today's Chinese are often using relationships in a wrong manner, which has resulted in lots of adverse effects. Many Chinese scholars take guanxi as an evil thing. And this has led to radical propositions. Some of these propositions say that laws can replace morality, and rigid punishment is enough to control Chinese misconducted behaviors. According to traditional Chinese wisdom, laws don't work alone, and that ruling under law is impossible to create social orders with the absence of morality. Laws are of course important. Since Chinese society is in transformation, there must be many areas where laws have yet to be enacted. It is therefore necessary to promulgate more laws. Nonetheless, it is impossible for laws to work without support from ethics. We are always calling for rule-of-law-based society, but western rule-of-law-based society is built upon ethics. The late American legal scholar Harold J. Berman believed that western legal system was built upon Christian ethics. In contrast, we seldom think about the following issue: What kind of ethics is needed for rule of law in China?

And other propositions advocate management based upon impersonal relationships. In reality, since the 1930s, a lot of leading experts in organizational theory have proved that the "impersonal relationships" in the principles of hierarchical control developed by Max Weber is nothing but a dream, as it is impossible for them to exist. How then can we take this dream as the panacea for management?

Weber is mostly criticized by the other experts in organizational theory in that hierarchy is of course effective, but that there must be a group of people, the decision makers, whose work cannot be restricted by processes, regulations and formal institutions. Given the changeability and high uncertainties of their work, they have access to considerable freedom beyond institutions and control the entire systems of processes and orders. The more successful the hierarchy control, the more centralized to higher levels the power. The aftermath of centralized power include corruption, the abuse of power, and the tendency of the power holder to expand his power, which leads to greater power. Impersonal relationships turn employees into atomized individuals who are fully exposed to control under organizational violence. This in turn results in further centralized and expanded power and, in the end, the unsustainability of such a system.

And there are also propositions, mostly from some economists, that the old ethics should be superseded by some new ethics. These economists believe that the new ethics centers on the honoring of contracts in the market and that the old ethics is among friends. It seems that transaction relations can be used to replace all expressive ties. They are unaware that the primary interpersonal ties are expressive rather than instrumental. All moralities, including Ren (often translated as "humaneness") developed by Confucius, Yi (often translated as "reciprocity") developed by Mencius, and philanthropy instituted by Jesus Christ, aim to regulate expressive ties more than they do to instrumental ties, not to mention the buyer-seller relationship, which represents only a small portion of human relationships. Do we really hope that someday, there is no friendship, affection or ethics among human beings and that the buyer-seller relationship covers even marriage?

The real problems that face China today include greediness and eagerness for instant success and profits. And the Unites States is also faced with similar moral deterioration, which is doubtlessly exemplified by the violation of laws and regulations. That is why there have been a series of cases such as accounting fraud by Enron Corporation and Arthur Andersen LLP (it was one of the world's "Big Five" accounting firms) together; fat cats in Wall Street designed toxic assets and triggered a financial tsunami. In the case of China, greediness and eagerness for instant success and profits are always exemplified by the use of relationships, which causes societal problems such as corruption, under table trade, back-door favor exchanges and the manipulation of guanxi. But all these should be blamed not on rule of law, in the United States, and guanxi-orientation, in China, but on eagerness for short-term profits, greediness, and over-ambitiousness. In other words, today China's problem is not caused by "guanxi society", and rather it comes from the lack of cultivating self—the starting point of guanxi management.

Lecture 4 Dynamics of Guanxi

The first idea I want to discuss in this lecture is that China is a guanxi society, where the basic structure of its social behaviors contains elements, such as networking based on family-ethics, differential modes of association, grouping in the form of ego-centered circle and thinking of dynamic balance, that remain changeless in a very long period of Chinese history. However, Chinese gradually change what is included in their family-ethics based relations and the way how to develop these relations, following the trend of an evolving and increasingly mobile society as well as expanding cities, thereby adapting to the ever-changing society. This evolution is actually about things other than the essential elements in China.

The basic structure of governance also remains changeless in Chinese society. The Chinese old saying says: "the emperor's power is as far as the heaven"; that means, there is a large room for self-organization in the gross-root society which is out of bureaucratic control. Self-organization comes from the phenomenon of guanxi circles among Chinese, and circles result from relationship networks in the differential mode of association, with their norms including a set of principles of favor exchanges; and this set of principles in turn derive from family ethics. And all these have become the code of conduct for Chinese thanks to the omnipresent philosophy of Confucianism. In contrast with the changeless underlying structure of these relationships in Chinese society, their contents are changeable, that is, who will be regarded as familiar or even pseudo-family ties?

4.1 Historical Changes in the Contents of Relationships

China was known as "ten thousand domains" in the far ancient times, when a phratry could become a small domain. The kings of Zhou Dynasty were known as "the common king of the world", that is, a large number of small domains submitted to the same king, but actually they were independent from the common king. During the early Spring and Autumn period (BC. 770-476), there were still over three thousand domains in China. These domains were gradually merged during fighting with each other till they turned into seven major states in the Warring States period. The Qin Dynasty went further to unify China into a single whole. In this process, the meanings and scopes of "family" and "state" kept changing. In the early Western Han Dynasty (BC. 202-AD. 9), a relationship system based on the Confucian family ethics was established under the theory of a great scholar, Dong Zhongshu. It was in this period that order based on "three principles" (in Chinese, three-Gong, i.e. three basic types of relations) and "Let the ruler be a ruler, minister be a minister, father be a father, son be a son" was initially established; a minister served his king just like a son served his father. These changes indeed included the minister-king, or subordinate-supervisor, relationship into family ties.

The phenomenon of blood brothers emerged in the late Eastern Han Dynasty （AD. 25-220）. The "three blood brothers (i.e., Liu Bei, Guan Yu and Zhang Fei) in the peach orchard" has since become a well-known legend. The phenomenon of family ties resulting from blood brothers became increasingly obvious till it reached the highest level in the Jin dynasties (AD. 265-420), when main clans were so powerful that important appointments made by the emperor of the Eastern Jin Dynasty (the second half of Jin Dynasty) could not become valid until they were consented to by those clans. In addition to monopoly on the appointment of government officials, the clans were running a large-scale estate economy in which they adopted homeless persons, who then became tenant farmers working for the clans. Intellectuals from poor families could establish relationships with the clans by submitting visiting cards. Thus, the adoption system and a new type of pseudo-family ties emerged in this period.

The adoption system became best developed in the Tang Dynasty. An Lushan, a general who rebelled against the Tang Dynasty, claimed to have three thousand adopted sons, who were all orphans from nomadic peoples in northern and western China and later on became the most loyal part of An's rebellion army. Another well-known example about the adoption system was Li Keyong, a Shatuo (a Turkic tribe) military governor during the late Tang Dynasty, and thirteen warriors. These warriors were actually adopted sons of Li Keyong, to whom they were very loyal and ultimately helped his natural son Li Cunxu found Later Tang Dynasty. Prevailing in the Tang Dynasty, the adoption tradition can still be seen in today's Japan, where lots of family businesses have a habit of appointing the adopted sons of their leaders to leading positions.

The greatest changes in the meaning of "Guanxi" in China occurred in the Spring and Autumn period and the Song Dynasty (AD. 960-1276). Chinese society changed greatly in the Song Dynasty, when commerce and trading were well developed and business taxes exceeded agricultural ones for the first time in Chinese history. The highly developed commerce and trading led to a greater society and, hence, had a significant impact on traditional family and societal forms. It was under this background that Fan Zhongyan, a prominent politician and literary figure in the Song Dynasty, created donated farmland system so as to make clans cohesive again. The donated farmland (including the fields, mountains and woods owned by a clan) was an asset of the entire clan and was typically bought by the richest family in this clan. To protect the clan's farmland from being privatized, it was usually required that the farmland be cultivated not by people of the clan's surname but by employed tenant farmers of other names, and that the levied land tax be for use by the clan. Nonetheless, the membership of a clan gradually changed with time, as what used to be a large clan could decline into a very small one. In the meantime, the number of tenant farmers gradually increased till they became an integral part of the village. And the meaning of clan changed in this context. The families of different surnames, which lived together, might look for their common ancestry and merged into a single clan that worshiped their ancestry in the sample temple. Anthropologist Zhang Xiaojun referred to this phenomenon as "self-created clans." It was in this situation that the meaning of clan changed to include more than groups of people with real blood relationships. And that was how egocentric guanxi networks, especially the rings of family and familiar ties, further expanded in China. This constituted the base for townsmen in the later process of commerce development. Geo-relationship became critical.

In the Ming Dynasty, there were a growing number of regional groups of businesses based on geo-relationships. Friendship spanning two or more generations – if two persons are good friends, then their children may marry each other and their brotherhood will be passed down to the subsequent generations – also became increasingly important, and Chinese entered another era. If a person in such friendship was unable to repay a debt, then he could be exempted from the debt by kneeling down and bowing so low as to have his head knock the ground several times before the creditor. This movement signified that "I will remember this favor forever."

Friendship between blood brothers became increasingly important as industry and commerce were well developed and life in cities became better in the period since the Song and Ming dynasties. The Chinese population topped one hundred million persons in the Song Dynasty and reached two hundred persons in the Ming Dynasty, before hitting the mark of four hundred million in the mid-Qing Dynasty. There were no major breakthroughs in production technologies in this period, but changes in management techniques brought a great increase in productivity. This is what Mark Elvin referred to as "economic growth without technological progress." The innovation in management techniques specifically refer to the mode in which big suppliers dealt with vendors who in turn sold goods to family workshops, in which men did farming while women did weaving, and in which the workshop was immediately behind the storefront. This mode led to today's network-like structure dominant in Chinese enterprises. Urbanization was also a characteristic of this period, but it differed from the current urbanizations in that, instead of big cities at present, there were then a large number of prosperous small towns, which became the hubs of vendors. A mobile population and urbanization both made friendship increasingly important; emphasis on Yi (i.e., brotherhood or reciprocity) and Guan Yu (the symbol of Yi; he is a general serving under the warlord Liu Bei in the legend of three blood brothers in the peach orchard) worship also began to prevail from this period onward.

It is in the present period that another round of major relationship changes has occurred in the process of Chinese modernization. This was what I gradually felt when I was doing field study on governance over outsourcing services. I compared Taiwan-based traditional companies (in the textile industry) with high-tech ones (in PC manufacturing) in terms of network form of organization, before I found obvious differences between them. Firstly, the sources of outsourcing relationships in the PC industry are no longer originated from expressive ties, as relationships are now mostly established with partners invited in an open manner in the market. Secondly, trust no longer derives from favor exchanges or daily social interactions, but is from long-term cooperation and the resulting tacit understanding. With regard to relationship development, therefore, everything ranging from control mechanism and daily management to relationship review is made in an institution-based manner. However, when partnership was built, Chinese tend to add expressive elements in to strengthen it.

When it comes to relationships among Chinese, a big difference between the present and the past is that relationships are more likely from friendship than from family, townsmen or clans; and partnership is more likely developed from strangers with common friends than from townsmen or multi-generation friendship. Outsourcing service providers are from two main sources. Firstly, the classmates or peers of leading designers in the company usually know relevant persons and hence are able to recommend outsourcing service providers. Accordingly, connections in your profession, industry and school become crucial. Secondly, relationships are established through formal plus informal institutions. First of all, you learn about the service quality and the reputation of relevant outsourcing service providers from your friends in various associations, such as ball game clubs, the federation of industry and commerce and the Taiwanese merchant association in Mainland China. And you ask your friends for recommendations. After that, you send an assessor team to assess the service quality and reliability of the recommended outsourcing service provider, before ultimately deciding whether to partner with him or not. Briefly, this is a process where governance is carried out with formal institutions plus favor exchanges.

And although the two parties to an outsourcing service are not familiar with each other at the beginning, they will gradually work together more often as long as they think that the other party is trustworthy. On the one hand, if the buyer finds a less expensive outsourcing service provider during cooperation with the current one, he usually will not replace the latter immediately. Instead, he will negotiate with the current outsourcing service provider and, whenever necessary, help the latter reduce the costs to enable him to lower the price, thereby maintaining the current partnership whenever possible. On the other hand, the outsourcing service provider typically will receive a growing number of orders and represent an increasing share of the total business contracted out by the buyer as long as the provider behaves in a trustworthy manner. Along with the upgrade of partnership, private friendship generally grows. And the buyer usually will give the provider more personal advises. As a result, the provider may be able to expand the cooperation from products such as casings to others and even form a regional group of businesses to make investment together. Such is the case often seen in many Chinese enterprises, such as Taiwan- and Wenzhou-based businesses.

As a result of this phenomenon, a company tends to have a bureaucracy to control a network of comparatively independent subunits, or alternatively, form numerous networks of outsourcing service providers around it (or both, for a lot of companies), after it reaches a certain size. And outsourcing service providers sometimes also contact each other to carry out parallel outsourcing services in order to rapidly respond to changeable needs. They may ultimately form a regional group of businesses to make investment together or even engage in the politics of lobbying.

As a second result, Chinese pay increasing attention to establishing ties with strangers on the basis of their trustworthy behavior, before becoming closer with them. Since transactions in the hi-tech industry are made in an increasingly frequent manner together with higher professional requirements, it is very difficult for people to find partners from townsmen, multi-generation friendship and extended kinship relations. As they become closer with strangers, the latter ones will develop into acquaintance ties with whom they will make a growing number of favor exchanges and transactions, before developing further into familiar ties and members of their circles. This will obviate the selection of partners from among a very small number of candidates. Westerners are inclined to segment a chain of complex transactions into increasingly fine granularity so as to turn them, as many as possible, into short-term, less complex, more certain transactions that ultimately will be made in a market-oriented manner. By comparison, Chinese are inclined, once trust is built, to make bilateral cooperation increasingly complex and diverse in terms of contents and modes, in addition to making them longer, before ultimately carrying it out on the basis of friendship networks.

4.2 Dynamic Relationship Changes

Familiar ties generally exist among friends and, as mentioned above, can develop gradually from acquaintance ties instead of members of clans or townsmen. Nonetheless, Chinese often partner with their family or pseudo-family members to make strong instrumental exchanges. In Chinese family businesses, for example, father and son, husband and wife, and brothers tend to become business partners. Moreover, circle members deriving from among family members differ from the ones from acquaintances in that the former ones contain more expressive exchanges and require higher family-ethics. By comparison, as is believed by sociologist Yang Yi-Yin, family ties mixed with instrumental exchanges are less dependent upon affection than are pure family ties, because the rational calculation of personal gains and bargaining will both weaken the affection in expressive ties. In addition, indigenous psychologist Hwang, Kwang-Kuo believes that Chinese are inclined to improve expressive feels while developing strong instrumental ties. Since there are many things that acquaintances have no chance to do, it is necessary to enhance the expressive elements so as to develop the ties with them into familiar ties. Only after that is it possible to make stronger, instrumental exchanges.

By combining the ideas of the two scholars, I proposed a structure for analyzing relationships among Chinese under the instrumental and expressive dimensions, and divided each dimension into strong and weak relationship categories. The model of the four relationship categories built upon these two dimensions is as following figure:

According to this diagram of the path along with interpersonal relationships change, the relationships among Chinese, in this model, can be explained from the instrumental and expressive dimensions. The two dimensions are the two axes, of which the instrumental dimension is characterized by the equity rule and the expressive dimension by the need rule. The relationships at the lower left corner involve acquaintances and obey the equity rule; family ties are at the lower right corner and focus on the need rule.

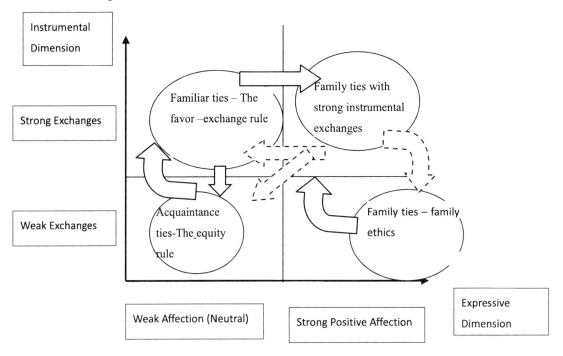

Figure 4.1 The Diagram of Guanxi Dynamics

Familiar ties combine the former two types by paying equal attention to the principles of equity and need, that is, they obey the favor-exchange rule. There are two different types of familiar ties in this model. Familiar ties built upon acquaintances are in the upper left quarter and are close to the middle line vertical to the axis of abscissa. They realize, under the favor rule, certain instrumental exchanges and lead to deeper expressive ties. By comparison, family ties with strong instrumental exchanges are in the upper right quarter that is close to the middle line vertical to the axis of abscissa. They reflect the assumption that as instrumental exchanges increase, family ties become less expressive.

Accordingly, the arrows in solid lines show the possible path of relationship changes. Building family ties with strong instrumental exchanges is also very risky. Firstly, maintaining such ties takes high expressive and instrumental costs. Secondly, once such ties no longer exist, it will be very difficult to reenter purely expressive family ties and even to maintain acquaintance ties, thereby resulting in negative or even no ties. In addition, the arrows in dashed lines signify that such relationship changes do not exist.

How then do Chinese dynamically change these ties?

4.2.1 From Strangers to Acquaintance Ties: Nine Similarities and Identification

Next, let's explain how these ties change with several observed cases.

In the first case, the process in which the president of CL Industrial Ltd., or Mr. A, relied on universities to virtualize the company and made it go through a crisis fully demonstrates how to build acquaintance ties through "identification" and let them function through instrumental exchanges.

Founded in 1994, CL Industrial Ltd. is in the environmental industry and provides products mainly including oil and water separators and oil interceptors for small to big restaurants, industrial-purpose mineral/light oil and water separators and high-speed leftover fermenters. CL Industrial has its own processing equipment, a headcount of about twelve employees and an annual fixed operating cost of about six to seven million yuan (the Chinese dollar). It was making losses in the 2000-2001 period due to depression and heavy pressure from bank loans. Fortunately, Mr. A was very diligent, open to new knowledge, quick-witted and good at making friends. And he made friends in a very special way – he took delight in sharing his expertise and life experience with others. A professor with the MZ University of Technology learned from Formosa Plastics Group (FPG) – CL Industrial was one of its partners – which CL Industrial specialized in fermenters, so he asked Mr. A for expertise on leftover fermenters. Given their common interests in environmental technologies, Mr. A shared all his expertise with the professor. As they talked, both of them increasingly felt the possibility of cooperation. So they did research together. Later on, they managed to secure a 5,000,000-yuan research subsidy.

There is actually a very important source of relationships – common friends – in addition to the "nine tungs" (similarities) we have discussed above. It may be referred to as "the tenth tung"—the common friend. Chinese most often say, when trying to establishing relationships with others, that "You know Jack? We've been good friend for xx years …" We can see, therefore, that common friends are a good medium for establishing minimum trust.

We have all acted as someone who introduces one of our friends to another so as to enable an exchange between them. The introducer plays dual roles – the mediator and the assurer.

To virtualize CL Industrial, the above-mentioned president rapidly contacted the incubation center of the MZ University of Technology thanks to recommendation by the above-mentioned professor. This university provided CL Industrial with big office space, good office equipment, labs and sufficient research HR. Later on, it also employed, for its canteens, oil interceptors produced by CL Industrial. This was a win-win situation between the company and the university resulting from an instrumental exchange. Backed by FPG and the university together, Mr. A was better able to persuade others when carrying out marketing events. The company has seen its annual fixed cost decrease to somewhere between 700,000 and 900,000 yuan after the virtualization. Three years after that, it has not only paid off the debts, but has also increased the gross margin to 20-30%.

Another case was from SF Technologies Co., Ltd. founded in 2001. Specializing high-tech clean room design and supervision over manufacturing, it has customers across the Taiwan Strait, including AU Optronics Corp. (AUO), Wintek, Winbond, Forhouse, H.P.B. Optoelectronics, and Corning and, on the side of the Chinese Mainland, Fortech Optronics (Xiamen) Co., Ltd, United Win Technology Limited, Dongguan Masstop and China Resources Microelectronics Limited. SF Technologies started up with an order worth only 80,000 yuan. The acquisition of this order, plus the subsequent expansion of the corporate business, demonstrates the president's capabilities of establishing relationships with others. The president of SF Technologies, or Mr. B, before joining the company, ran a travel agency and had a habit of playing badminton, by which he made a lot of friends. In 2001, one of such friends who worked at Wintek and who had known him for three years told him that there was a small project within the company and asked if he was interested in it or not. In that period of time, people were suffering a sharp decrease of their wealth due to the   bubble in the stock market, especially in the hi-tech investment, so they were unwilling to travel. Since it was difficult to continue his travel business, Mr. B wanted to make a change in his career. He then partnered with his brother, who worked for an air conditioner maker, to found SF Technologies and received their first ever order from Wintek. At that time, Wintek was also building a facility, so it had small or large projects very often. Mr. B spent half a day at Wintek almost every day and, later in the period of cooperation, it looked like he had a small office at Wintek. Since he was in the service industry before this, Mr. B was fully aware of the importance of customer service and satisfaction. He then introduced some service quality-centric ideas and practices into the new company and doubled as a project supervisor to assure good project quality and responsiveness. And he soon established ties with most employees and low-level managers of Wintek's engineering department, which was in the same field as was his company, in the capacity as an outsourcing service provider for Wintek.

We can see from the above example that a Chinese person generally would not act as an introducer for someone else unless they have a sufficiently good tie with each other, because the introducer needs to take part of the resulting risks. Introduction, therefore, can also be regarded as a type of favor exchanges. Next, let us discuss familiar ties and favor exchanges.

4.2.2 From Acquaintance Ties to Familiar Ties: The Principles of Requital and Favor

Acquaintance tis' turning into good friends is a process that relies on favor exchanges and that often involves ceremonial acts, such as often having dinner together after work, calling each other "Buddy", etc. Such expressive acts in China, however, are no more than a declaration that "I invite you to be my buddy." By this time, the two persons are not yet real friends. Acquaintance tis' turning into familiar ties entails a large number of favor exchanges, which, as we have mentioned above, have several characteristics. Firstly, they are a type of debts of gratitude that the giver is not allowed to talk about while the receiver must not forget. Secondly, they are a type of long-term acts – people keep doing somebody a favor on the one hand and doing something in return of somebody else's favor on the other. Thirdly, there are always favor debts in each one's favor account. Fourthly, they are highly need-specific, as they are always intended to satisfy an individual's urgent and particular need, such as providing critical resources or helping to make face.

"Making face" is something very interesting in China. Businesspersons, for example, typically like inviting governmental officials to conferences or seeking to have photos taken with them before putting them up on the walls in their offices. Either of them actually means the endorsement from these officials. These are typical instances of making face. On the other hand, making face usually requires "returning face", that is, doing things in return of the favor debts. Such businesspersons, again for example, tend to hold a grand banquet and invite people from different sectors to it on the birthday of one of the aforementioned government officials or their parents. This is how they demonstrate their extensive ties. This is essentially a type of favor exchanges: I help you make face today to prove that I'm within your guanxi circle and, on some other day, you speak for me to show your support. This is a favor that requires reward in one way or another in the long run although it is impossible to clearly price it.

The circle theory that I will try to put forward next focuses on this proposition: Chinese always attempt to change short-term transactions into long-term favor exchanges. As relationships are established, the scope of favor exchanges generally will keep expanding. Westerners are inclined to carry out short-term transactions; and Chinese, long-term cooperation. Moreover, favor exchanges have a fifth quality that they are made in an extremely wide scope plus very rich contents. A group of businesspersons, for example, may at first carry out no more than simple cooperation, such as Jack buying yarn from Tom. As their relationship grows deeper, however, their cooperation will probably go beyond this. Gradually, Jack also may buy from Tom buttons needed by his factory. They may become long-term partners and join the same regional group of businesses, before ultimately making investment, speculating in the housing market and even carrying out political lobbying together.

When people establish familiar ties with each other, expressive acts are no more than ceremonial, so to speak, as they are only symbolic invitation. And only after real essential benefits are exchanged will their relationships be increasingly cemented. Friends will become increasingly distant with each other if they can find no reason for such exchanges. And many years later, when they meet again, they will see it very difficult to find anything in common, especially in terms of interests, despite that they remain emotionally close to each other.

Next, I would like to use several examples to explain the process of guanxi management while acquaintance ties are developing into familiar ties. Mr. A of CL Industrial, again for example, got to know a businessperson whose company produced high-grade knitting paper. His products were amazingly beautiful and had extensive applications. Mr. A once again shared his expertise with this businessperson, told the latter of some business opportunities that could be developed, and, hence, helped the latter increase the sales revenue greatly. So the two persons gradually turned into familiar ties from acquaintances. A subsequent favor exchange brought closer ties between them. A five-star hotel invited a high-ranking government official to announce its opening; how to package the gift for this official became a headache of its executives. After knowing this problem, Mr. A sent them a package and a handbag made of knitting paper produced by the aforementioned businessperson's company. All the attendees, on the day of the ceremony, couldn't help marveling at the package, and many of them later on asked where such a refined package and handbag came from. By acting as an introducer, Mr. A helped the businessperson win not only business opportunities, but also good word of mouth in the industry and ties with high-ranking government officials. It was with such a positive cycle of favor exchanges that the two persons established good familiar ties with each other. They were not only good friends, but also became partners in many business deals.

And on the side of Mr. B of SF Technologies, the building of familiar ties was more about wisdom and skills in selecting from among candidates for these ties. Two years after Mr. B started his business, the Central Taiwan Science Park (CTSP) was founded and received an influx of big companies that came here to build facilities. By that time, there had been few high-tech companies in central Taiwan, and Wintek was one of them. New comers that needed specialist in the field of clean rooms all attempted to poach such specialists from Wintek through high salaries. And many of the Wintek employees who had good personal relations with Mr. B joined the new comers and played important roles there. Some of them were even transferred to the Chinese Mainland. These persons, who already were friends of Mr. B, of course recommended SF Technologies to their new employers. Accordingly, SF Technologies saw its operating income multiply in addition to business presence across the Taiwan Strait. Behind this seemingly smooth process was a philosophy unique to Mr. B in terms of operating egocentric guanxi network. Firstly, cultivate people in a peer-to-peer manner. This should start from the middle level managers and even the grass roots instead of the top level. That is because you can receive immediate benefits by approaching the high-ranking managers, but you will find it very difficult to establish long-term familiar ties with them. Mr. B said that there had long been sycophants around an executive, who would also think that these people were good to gain advantage and, accordingly, would take all such favors for granted. As a result, joining these sycophants generally will not bring you any advantage. This shows the difficulty of establishing ties with high-ranking officials before turning them into acquaintances and then into good friends. But the story with those at lower levels would be totally different, as they are short of resources and need to perform so well as to get promoted. Mr. B was therefore very friendly to such people. He would always do his best to help them solve problems at work in addition to inviting them to dinner and giving low-value gifts during holidays. That was how he enabled them to perform well before their superiors and within their companies and, thus, added to the favors that they owed to him.

Secondly, let people rely on you. Mr. B values the quality of services by doing a perfect job as long as it is within the company's service scope, thereby winning the other party's full trust. As time went by, these people would come to rely on Mr. B and always think of him whenever they had problems. And naturally, Mr. B would receive orders very smoothly. Later on, when these people at lower levels got promoted or joined other companies, they would still trust and rely on him. Today, SF Technologies are achieving successes one after another thanks to so many high-ranking officials with whom Mr. B has established close ties years before.

There may be people who doubt the capacity and power of minor roles, thinking that they have no say for major matters. Developing familiar ties will of course be useful for the future, but what about the present? This Mr. B would not deny, but he thinks that it is impossible for a company to only make big deals. It is true that high-ranking officials typically play a dominant role in the reception of big orders, but they tend to invite bids for such orders in an open manner. Accordingly, the candidates will compete with each other in terms of price and cost, and accordingly will make thin profits despite large monetary amounts. Briefly, receiving a big order does not always mean high margins. By comparison, small deals and orders tend to bring high margins despite small monetary amounts. Moreover, information on them is mostly possessed by minor roles. And that is how Mr. B gains access to massive information on small orders and does business with a nibble-away tactic, which, in the long run, will also bring considerable profits.

4.2.3 From Familiar Ties to Family Ties

It is even harder to turn friends into "family members", i.e. pseudo-family ties. Since there are, after all, interests-based exchange relationships between the two sides, certain ceremonial acts are generally needed, in addition to getting emotionally closer to the other side, so as to place those relationships into the field of "families" accepted by social norms, thereby turning them into family ties under the interests-irrelevant need rule. There are generally three most important ceremonial acts – marriage, adoption and becoming blood brothers.

There are three approaches, since the ancient times, to developing familiar ties into family ties in China. The first approach is marriage. There was a tradition in China that two children – one was supposed to be a boy and the other a girl – were engaged to each other even before they were born. And this was intended to get the two families so close as to become a single one. The second approach is adoption, which reached the peak in the Tang Dynasty（AD. 581-907）. The phenomenon of adoption remains common in Japan where much of the Tang culture is retained. The third approach, or the one that later on became most prevalent in China, was becoming blood brothers. And this phenomenon was most common in the Song Dynasty (960-1279) . At this time, merchants from Shanxi Province emphasized the idea of "Rely on friends when away from home" since they kept traveling in a dynasty with flourishing industry and commerce. It was also at this time that Guan Yu（the most famous general in the Three-Kingdom period, AD. 220-280）worship began to emerge from among these merchants and, later on, spread to more people thanks to his loyalty to Liu Bei（Guan Yu's blood brother and supervisor）. I refer to the "family members" in this context as "pseudo-family ties" since they are not confined to the same ancestry, surname or army. Like in the case of real family members, the family ethics applies to pseudo-family ties.

The first company has, CL Industrial as we have said above, transformed itself into a virtual business marketing platform that specializes in design and services. Nonetheless, how can a virtual company that has contracted out the entire manufacturing and processing business control product quality, lead time, costs and services? Chinese SMEs are globally renowned for flexibility and low costs resulting from networks of partners. Unfortunately, however, the SMEs in such networks are less loyal than are Japanese companies, as they sometime prioritize costs over anything else and partner with whichever makes the lowest offer. Consequently, all of them are involved in price competition that leads to a continuous decrease in gross margins and, ultimately, even the final winners will be struggling, not to mention making big money.

The aforementioned virtual company had an outsourcing service provider as one of its partners. With excellent technologies, timely delivery, honesty and diligence, this provider was the one with which this company worked most often and had the closest ties. But he had a relatively high cost of outsourcing services despite the best quality. The provider had a beautiful daughter, say, Mary, for example, who then majored in music and was always his pride. By the time when Mary graduated with a master's degree, the provider played, for Mr. A, the DVD of her public music performance. Seeing such an elegant and cultured girl, Mr. A couldn't help praising her within himself. Three years later, the youngest son, say, Peter, for example, of Mr. A got to know the girl at an exhibition as part of the World Expo. Later on, the provider met Peter at the banquet as part of the wedding of Mr. A's eldest son. He felt that Peter knew just how to deal with others and was mature and polite. Since neither Mary nor Peter was in love with anyone, they began dating with blessings from their parents and later on, as were expected by all, married.

In the story above, it took four years for the two parties to turn from acquaintances into familiar ties and then into family members. When it comes to developing relationships with the provider, the patience of Mr. A is visible in addition to luck. Since they already worked with each other closely before the marriage, it is predictable that the provider works, after the marriage, as the only outsourcing service provider for Mr. A's company, which has even contracted out the after-sales service to the former. And the company also has transformed itself smoothly into a marketing platform and design service provider with low costs and high margins. Marriage aimed at deepening ties similar to the aforementioned ones has of course become less common, nowadays, than becoming blood brothers.

4.2.4 Damages to Relationships

It is difficult, as we have said above, to establish family ties with strong instrumental exchanges, and it is also costly to withdraw from them. This has been fully demonstrated by the story of DoubleStar, which was China's leading sports shoe brand. A fight for ownership of the group broke out between Wang Hai, the President of the group, and a couple, Liu Shuli and Han Junzhi, who are his nominal son and nominal daughter respectively, in April 2008.

It is beyond question that Wang Hai had built a loving and effective home-like context for this couple, as he had granted them a high power for internal contracting and, hence, allowed the realization of their individual interests largely go beyond restrictions of the collective. The new market-oriented restructuring and reform, however, reclaimed all their powers suddenly and thoroughly. This let them feel that they had been deprived of what they deserved and been improperly treated. These feelings were stronger than the sense of belong to the collective. And that was how the family ties and mutual trust, which they had strenuously built, broke up. Not only was it impossible for both sides to maintain the partnership, but there were even wars of words and prices between them as competitors to each other in the market, let alone maintain any positive tie.

This case enables us to see why it is very difficult to turn the family ties with strong instrumental exchanges in the third phase in the figure 4.1, once they break up, into the ones in any other phase. It is impossible for the involved parties to return to the original expressive ties and difficult even to be like general acquaintances. Instead, they are like strangers or even enemies.

To avoid such breakup of ties, Chinese always emphasize two things: business is business even if you are dealing with your real family members; it is always advisable to define rules before you make a deal with someone else. Partnerships, if they are short of an effective governance mechanism, pseudo-family ties are also prone to become problematic. The DoubleStar case, once again, lets us see the necessity of governing an organization under rituals and laws together. It was delays in initiating governance under formal rules that made the DoubleStar Group become an example of failure.

4.3 Characteristics of Chinese Management – Flexibility and Quick Response

Familiar ties, among all the types of ties, deserve extra attention. It is these ties that make Chinese value long-term guanxi contracts rather than short-term transactional contracts. This quality has led to the essence of Chinese management. While comparing high-tech industries with the relatively traditional model that one town focuses on one industry (e.g., the small-machinery or textile industry), I found out that townsmen, clans or long-time friends would become less important in global markets or industries with relatively high technological barriers. Instead, familiar ties that evolved from relationships with business partners recommended by friends would become critical.

I still remember that I asked a Taiwanese high-tech industry researcher in an interview with the latter: Why neither Japan nor Korea was as good as us in the high-tech ODM (original design manufacturing) field? Was the labor cost really the most important factor? He replied that the labor cost did not necessarily represent a high share of the total cost of high-tech manufacturing, that it depended on specific products, and that it represented a very small share of the total cost of chip manufacturing, for example. In reality, our advantages include:

(1) We are extremely flexible and, hence, are able to rapidly adjust the output, making us most suitable for industries with great business cycle fluctuations;

(2) We are quickly responsive. There was a period when it took Japan at least two or three weeks to trial-manufacture a high-tech product, as opposed to seven days in China. Today, this time has even been reduced to three days.

Both flexibility and responsiveness, which are most emphasized by recent western management theories, have actually had good practices in China.

Back in the 1990s when China was still relative poor, management guru Peter Drucker predicted that Chinese must have managerial wisdom to share with the rest of the world. A dozen of years later, however, we have yet to see indigenous management theories developed by any Chinese scholar in management, and do not even know where they are supposed to go. By comparison, Bill Fischer, Professor of Innovation Management at IMD Business School in Lausanne, Switzerland, gained an onlooker's insight, saying that China indeed has contributed to the world in terms of management and its contribution is about how to organize and lead to 'faster-paced operations.' Speed is now critical, and it is an undisputable fact that the Chinese economy is the world's fastest at both the macro and the micro levels. He argues that Chinese employees in multinationals can easily catch up with their foreign colleagues when implementing new projects or finishing tasks successfully through cooperation among multiple parties that pursue the common goal.

Responsiveness, flexibility and multi-party cooperation – these indeed are the strengths of Chinese business managers. Unfortunately, indigenous scholars fail to notice them despite that they have every chance to observe them, on the one hand, or can find no theory to explain them, on the other.

After eighteen years of field study on enterprises, I have realized that with regard to the reasons for Chinese enterprises' quick response and flexibility, it is necessary to learn about them from Guanxi management and network-like structures within these enterprises.

In 1994, when I came back from the United States where I had studied, I had in mind nothing but managerial knowledge I had learned there (including organizational theories when I studied social sciences, plus knowledge I learned when I was studying for a master's degree in the department of economics and a master's degree in industrial engineering in the department of applied mathematics). Kao, Cheng-shu, Professor at the Department of Sociology, Tunghai University in Taiwan, told me an interesting qualitatively observed case, when we first talked with each other about his research on East Asian economies. A foreign buyer came to Taiwan and visited the world's largest maker of motors for toys, which then represented 70% of global markets for such motors. The buyer thought that this must be a company with about 10,000 employees, modern factories and western managerial institutions. To his surprise, he came, after twists and turns (in the literal meaning), to a countryside-like place, where there were a group of old workshops and only more than 400 workers. The buyer could not believe that these workers were able to produce such a high output value. It was on that day that the company held a year-end banquet (a dinner to which the business owner invites the employees before Chinese New Year to thank them for their efforts in the past year), during which the buyer was suddenly enlightened. It turned out that there were about one hundred tables during the banquet, to which representatives of about one hundred suppliers were invited. The chairman of the motor maker toasted each table to strengthen the emotional ties with the guests. This let the foreign buyer realize how Chinese businesspersons maintained relationships with outsourcing service providers. Such a high output value, of course, was produced not by only four hundred employees, but by these employees and all the suppliers together. It was this case that urged me to reorient my research – I have since been using qualitative methods to research the structures of Chinese enterprises. And I have seen that they have a common structure: There is a hierarchy at the upper level of the organizational structure and a network at the lower level; there is a hierarchy inside an organization and a network outside. In other words, the core business of the company is controlled by a hierarchy-based organization, but there tend to be organizations operating in its name, branches as contractors of some other corporate businesses, or independent teams within the company; there usually is, outside it, a network of outsourcing service providers or a group of strategic partners; and more often than not, the company itself is part of a larger network such as a regional group of businesses or an industry cluster.

The hierarchy is responsible for the steady operation of the core business and management, while the network-like structure comprising a large number of independent or half-independent organizations is the very reason for Chinese enterprises to stay flexible and responsive.

How then can their managerial wisdom stay responsive in such a structure? Chinese high-tech manufacturers also are mostly operating under this structure, but why can they finish a job within only seven days while a Japanese conglomerate has to rely on an instruction system and spend two or three weeks to finish the same one? Remember that Chinese companies need to mobilize a huge network of outsourcing service providers in addition to the employees. How to manage the relationships with organizations operating in the name of the company, contractors, outsourcing service providers and allies? The answer lies somewhere in guanxi circle management within Chinese enterprises.

Lecture 5 Guanxi Circle– Why Chinese Want to Work

"The ancients, who wished to illustrate illustrious virtue throughout the world, first ordered well their own states. Wishing to order well their states, they first regulated their families. Wishing to regulate their families, they first cultivated themselves. Wishing to cultivate themselves, they first purified their minds. Wishing to purify their minds, they first sought to be sincere in their thoughts. Wishing to be sincere in their thoughts, they first extended to the utmost their knowledge. Such extension of knowledge lay in the investigation of things. Things being investigated, knowledge became complete. Their knowledge being complete, their thoughts were sincere. Their thoughts being sincere, their minds were then purified. Their minds being purified, their characters were cultivated. Their characters being cultivated, their families were regulated. Their families being regulated, their states were rightly governed. Their states being rightly governed, the whole world was made tranquil and happy."

—The Great Learning

In Lectures 1 and 2, I said that "The best leader is the leader who does nothing against nature" is at the core of Chinese managerial philosophies. In other words, jobs are done through natural self-organization. And according to the doctrine of dynamic balance, the cultivation of self-organization relies on guanxi management discussed in Lectures 3 and 4; it is intended to create an environment that enables harmony and trust inside and outside the organization. Only in this way is it possible to effectively connect independent self-organized units into a network of organizations so as to complete the entre value chain. Governing transactional relations across this chain, however, relies on the combination of rituals and rules, especially by building a vision and culture, developing informal regulations, and promoting mutual supervision within the network. These are the cornerstones for governance under rituals.

But why do Chinese have such self-organization-oriented managerial philosophies?

And why are such managerial philosophies able to enable qualities of Chinese management including being flexible, responsive and highly cooperative?

Next, I will try to answer these questions with the guanxi circle theory.

5.1 Explanations from Local Sociologists

What Francis L. K. Hsu referred to as "situation determinism" (Hsu, 1983) is an important principle regulating Chinese organizational behavior. As a Chinese attitude toward life, situation determinism is built upon relations among people who rely on each other and centers on family ethics to divide public and private spheres; people within and outside one's guanxi circle are treated in different ways; and norms vary with the situation. For the part of Chinese, an ideal family should be collectivistic; Confucian ethics requires individuals to obey the "three principles" (in Chinese, san gong) only at home. And Chinese will also expand the applicability of the code of conduct for families to their kin, clans, townsmen and even blood brothers and good friends. Accordingly, the guanxi circle of an individual is resizable, or elastic, depending upon the situation. Anybody, as long as he or she is within one's guanxi circle, will gain access to a share of benefits.

The leader of an organization will also manage people inside and outside his guanxi circle in different ways. Since his primary team members, or devoted followers, constitute the leader's core team, his relationships with them must contain instrumental exchanges and affection, and he also needs to show affection for them so as to create a sense of belonging to the "family." In this situation, exchanges between the members of the guanxi circle and the leader constitute a type of long-term guanxi contracts, under which they do not care about benefits or losses at particular times or places but pay more attention to the possibility of favor exchanges in a long period of time and in a large scope. In contrast, the business-is-business equity rule applies to officials and employees outside the guanxi circle, with exception to a few who receive special attention and are potential members of the guanxi circle. When dealing with these people, the leader can think less of favor exchanges and also can calculate benefits or losses at particular times or places.

5.2 The Relevant Theories in the West—From X to Z Theory

Since management is ultimately about managing people, different assumptions about the nature of man, or humanity, will lead to managerial theories that vary greatly from each other. There are now three mainstream theories: Theory X, Theory Y and Theory Z. Among them, theory X was developed by Douglas McGregor on the basis of a summary of previous assumptions about humanity in the field of management. He believed that the organizational design in his times were based on wrong assumptions: People hate to work; people are passive by nature; people object, again by nature, to reforms; people treat organizations with indifference; people need to be managed, etc. The main contents of Theory X can be summarized into:

(1) Most people are lazy and work as little as they can;
(2) Most people are not ambitious and prefer being led to assuming any responsibility;
(3) Most people have a personal goal that conflicts with the one of the organization; external

forces are required to realize the goal of the organization;

(4) Most people are irrational, unable to restrain themselves and prone to be affected;

(5) Most people will opt to do what brings the highest economic benefits so as to satisfy basic physical and safety needs;

(6) People can be grouped roughly into categories. Most people satisfy the aforementioned assumptions while only a small number of people can restrain themselves. The latter ones should assume managerial responsibility. Under Theory X, management focuses on directing and controlling employees. The Carrot and Stick Approach must be used to drive employees to work: Lure them with salaries, bonuses and benefits on the one hand and deter them with institutions and punishments on the other.

McGregor (McGregor, 1960) also argued that Theory X has wrong assumptions on humanity in that people are not born to hate work but can be self-motivated. And he then developed Theory Y. People can come to like working as long as they feel satisfaction and achievements at work, according to this theory. The main contents of Theory Y can also be summarized into:

(1) Most people are not born to dislike work, because work is as natural as games and rest. Work can be a type of satisfaction or punishment depending upon the context;

(2) External control and punishment are not the only method for urging people to work for the goal of the organization. They are even threats and obstacles to human beings and make them become mature at a slower pace. People are willing to carry out self-management and self-control to achieve the desirable objectives;

(3) There is no conflict between people's need for self-realization and the behavior required by the organization. With proper opportunities, they are able to make their individual goals consistent with that of the organization;

(4) Most people, under proper conditions, have learned not only to accept responsibility, but also to seek responsibility. Evading responsibility, lack of ambition and emphasis on the feeling of being safe usually result from experience rather than humanity;

(5) Most people, instead of the minority, are able to fully use their imagination, wisdom and creativity to solve challenging problems facing the organization;

(6) Most people, under conditions in the modern industry, can only use part of their potential wisdom.

It is based on these assumptions that Theory Y emphasizes that employees should be motivated in such a way that they can feel greater happiness and satisfaction at work. The main task for managers is creating a work environment that allows employees to unleash all their potential capabilities.

Japanese-American scholar William Ouchi criticized both theories mentioned above. Theories

X and Y are both based upon the individualistic American society and apply to American-style organizations (Type A) rather than collective Japanese organizations (Type J), according to Ouchi. In the 1980s, American organizations were faced with a several challenge from Japanese ones – the former ones were far behind the latter ones in terms of productivity. Ouchi compared the two types of organizations through empirical research and found out that: American companies were individualistic, so particular individuals made decisions and were responsible for the result; they had control and management methods that relied on written processes, institutions and regulations; the decision process was often characterized by the decision maker making a decision; the employment system was based largely upon short-term employment contracts; and performance assessment and promotion were mainly determined by superiors in a very fast way. By comparison, in collective Japanese organizations, decisions were made in a process of extensive participation with the need to seek consensus; the collective responsibility system was employed; control and management were carried out by means of hint-based control, that is, both jobs relied on governance under rituals characteristic of collectivism; instead of written regulations, people had a set of norms on which they had reached tacit agreement; and at the core was the lifetime employment system.

With the aforementioned research, Ouchi put forward the concept of Type J organization – a Japanese-style organizational model – on the basis of the managerial characteristics of Japanese organizations. With the addition of the managerial characteristics of American organizations, this led to Theory Z. This theory emphasizes employees' sense of belonging as the motive for work, and highlights how trust and the close inter-employee relations affect the productivity of an organization. Since the lifetime employment system is employed in Japanese organizations, employees feel, once they join the company, that they have entered a family and will never leave it. The employees therefore have a very strong sense of identification and belonging. Since the employees are very loyal to it, the company should provide them with a sense of belonging so that they feel like being at home. The lifetime employment system, slow assessment and promotion mechanisms, and specialty-irrelevant careers – all these make the employees bundle their lives tightly with that of the company once they join it, so they can do whatever is assigned to them and stay industrious to assure extremely high productivity. Seeking a sense of belonging and long-term employment is at the core of Theory Z.

It is interesting that a growing number of American companies seem to have begun practicing Theory Z after the 1980s. This includes long-term employment, emphasis on providing employees with a sense of belonging, 360° assessment on employees, etc. Nonetheless, all these companies denied, in a survey, that they did it because they were affected by Japanese companies. Instead, they believed that they gradually began these practices because they needed them. We can see, therefore, that the so-called managerial differences between cultures are actually not that obvious. It is not that only Theories X and Y apply to America, but that Theory Z may also apply to it, only to a lower extent.

If Theories X and Y were developed on the basis of managerial practices in the United States and Theory Z on those in Japan, what theory, then, should be developed on the basis of those in China? I refer to it as Theory of Circle, or Theory of Guanxi Circle. My statement that the guanxi circle theory applies to Chinese organizations does not suggest, of course, that Theories X, Y and Z are unimportant. Wages/salaries, bonuses, benefits and punishments are always important physical incentives, while a sense of belonging and identification absolutely is also a non-physical incentive needed by Chinese employees. The only difference lies in that there are things special important to incentives within Chinese organizations. Just like the contents of Theory Z can also been seen in American organizations, the phenomena of favor exchanges and guanxi circles also occur in organizations in America, Japan and many other countries, only that these characteristics are especially obvious in China.

5.3 The Guanxi Circle Theory

People often say that Chinese like building small circles (in Chinese, Xiao Chuan-Zi). In organizations, we, too, often say that Chinese like grouping. They suggest that a particular type of informal groups is extraordinarily important in Chinese organizations. I refer to it as the phenomenon of guanxi circles. What then is guanxi circle?

A guanxi circle consists of a group of people who come together for a common identity and benefits sharing. It may refer to a large community, such as those of engineers, travel mates, professors, etc. But it more often is a small group in which members know and interact with each other. The concept of "guanxi circle" in this text, or the so-called "small circle", refers to the one in the narrow sense, that is, it includes only small groups rather than large communities. A guanxi circle tends to have a focal person as the leader, so it may be called somebody's circle, such as Manager Zhang's circle or President Lin's circle. This means that an informal leader, whom I refer to as the focal person, forms a guanxi circle with people extraordinarily close to him or her. Members in this guanxi circle share common benefits and work together for them. In other words, the principle of "equal sharing" should be applied for all members of a circle.

Guanxi circles constitute an important part of the structure of Chinese society. As a result, Chinese organizations are full of informal groups that compete with each other for more resources of the organization, although sometimes they also work together to protect themselves when they are assessed by leaders at higher levels. This poses a tough challenge for the leaders of Chinese organizations.

Two important Chinese characteristics constitute the cultural and normative foundations for the phenomenon of guanxi circles. Firstly, just like the concept of "differential mode of association" put forward by the late local sociologist Fei Xiaotong (Fei, 1992), the ego-centered network of a Chinese person consists of guanxi circles at multiple rings, and different behavioral and moral standards apply to different relationships. Secondly, the "Yin and Yang" thinking in the process of organizational operations dominates two dynamic process of guanxi circle operations: A person may dynamically put a relationship into or remove it from his or her guanxi circle; if he or she is both the focal person of his or her guanxi circle and the leader in the organization, then to maintain harmony in a larger social network, he or she needs to balance interests inside and outside the guanxi circles.

Guanxi circles, or rather, small circles, at work usually develops from ego-centered social networks, which tend to comprise one focal person (or a group of focal persons, such as a couple, a pair of brothers, etc.) and only strong ties like his/her (or their) family ties (Chen, 1994; 1995) and familiar ties (Yang, 1993). That is why a guanxi circle can be named after a particular person, such as Manager Zhang's circle, Director Wang's circle or President Lin's circle. This concept is similar with "action sets" (Mayer, 1966) rather than "closed group" or "association." A guanxi circle is not a closed group, because it is ego-centered and loosely organized without fixed membership. The concept of "set" means a group of people who all have ties with the focal person and who have a known perimeter around them (Barnes, 1954). An action set comprises social connections mobilized intentionally by the focal person of a guanxi circle. This focal person aims to finish a series of actions for an individual or collective goal. As a type of action sets, guanxi circles are characterized by being groups that include only strong ties, i.e. family and familiar ties in the Chinese cultural context, and that carry out a series of long-lasting actions, such as finishing tasks, achieving objectives of the team/organization, competing for the organization's resources for one's own use and increasing its influence, etc.

Guanxi circles in Chinese organizations are very effective and efficient work units. With the strong motive of working with the other team members for future success, an actor stays loyal to the guanxi circle and has a sense of responsibility for it, whether it centers on him (or her) or not. It is common during guanxi circle operations, therefore, that a member works hard, assumes responsibility on his or her own initiative, shares resources and provides additional services within the guanxi circle. Outside it, however, he or she may be calculative and selfish, that is, he or she is seeking nothing but fairness in instrumental exchanges (Hwang, 1987; 1988).

Nonetheless, such an "internal group" is an ego-centered social network rather than a group of people with equal rights. Every actor may have a guanxi circle that differs from those of others, as it is built around him or her as an individual. But only those guanxi circles with a powerful leader as a center are real players in an organization. Since members within a guanxi circle have not only common, close ties, but also common interests, they need work together to fight for resources from the outside before sharing them. The continuity of their loyalty and friendship, therefore, is required for not only their respective long-term interests but also the collective interests. An actor, especially a power leader in an organization, indeed will build his or her guanxi circle as an informal group, team or subsidiary within the organization. Moreover, he or she will consider the special interests of his or her circle members when recruiting employees or giving rewards. In the meantime, he or she will rely on the members of his or her guanxi circle, in particular, to finish tasks. Within the guanxi circle, therefore, they pay more attention to maintaining their relations than to finishing a single task.

The guanxi circle of a Chinese consists of three rings, as is shown in the figure above, which constitute a resource mobilization mechanism with multiple levels of social capital. Acquaintances provide a lot of opportunities and resources, such as structural holes, information benefits and opportunities (Burt, 1992), which can be brought through weak ties. Nonetheless, resources in this ring cannot always be successfully mobilized.

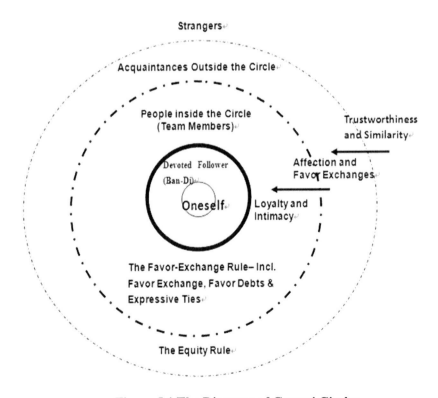

Figure 5.1 The Diagram of Guanxi Circles

The ring of family ties constitutes the most inner core of a person's guanxi circle. This core of a guanxi circle in the organizational field can be called "Ban-Di" (Chen, 1995), which means "the group of primary, loyal team members", "Qin-Xin" (Chi, 1996), which means "devoted followers", or, habitually in the Chinese Mainland, "Ban-Zi", which means the same as "Ban-Di", because these people constitute the primary force of the guanxi circle and have the closest ties with the focal person.

A group of good friends regarded as members of the guanxi circle act together as a buffer between the core of the guanxi circle and the world outside it. They are more flexible and open than those at the core and much better than acquaintances in terms of resource mobilization.

Like Theory Z, the guanxi circle theory emphasizes the sense of belonging and identification. The biggest difference between them lies in that employees are not collectivistic in an organization but are committed to a guanxi circle which is centered on one leader. And this leads to the phenomenon of guanxi circles that is especially prevalent in China. A Chinese person will seek the sense of belonging not in a company but in his or her guanxi circle. A successful corporate leader will try his or her best to turn the whole company into a guanxi circle, but in most companies, there are always numerous cliques. As a result, one of the very important motivations for Chinese to work is carrying out favor exchanges and joining others' guanxi circles to build up relationships, thereby creating their own guanxi circles.

5.4 The Motivations Behind Circle Members

5.4.1 Motive 1 – Favor Exchanges

When it comes to making personal achievements, Chinese always know that it is impossible for oneself to finish anything only by personal heroism. Accordingly, the more you want to succeed, the less you should act with heroism. Social relations that Chinese build up before starting favor exchanges are egocentric guanxi network. . To realize personal goals, Chinese will search the needed resources in their egocentric guanxi networks and, on the basis of the level of trust between each other, determine how many resources can be mobilized. Since such networks contain large amounts of resources, Chinese are fully aware that they need to rely on the power of a group of people to realize personal goals, and that sufficient resources are available for mobilization only if you keep building up relations. A person typically is in bad need of resources when he or she starts a business. In this period, Chinese will persevere quietly, work hard and do others favors so as to carry out favor exchanges and build up relations.

An important rule of conduct for Chinese is what Francis L. K. Hsu referred to as the "situation determinism" thinking. With family ethics being the rule of conduct, Chinese always identify persons inside or outside their guanxi circles depending upon their relationships with the latter ones; and they treat the latter ones under different rules of conduct. Chinese always know who are inside or outside their guanxi circles, and are able to adapt them to the situation.

Chinese will also expand the applicability of the code of conduct for "families" to their kin, clans, townsmen and even blood brothers and good friends. Accordingly, the guanxi circle of an individual is resizable, or elastic, depending upon the situation. The collectivism-oriented code of conduct for families applies to members of a guanxi circle, not to those outside it. In China, excellent professionals may work overtime and do many additional jobs without complaint so as to carry out long-term favor exchanges and, ultimately, join "the guanxi circles."

For the part of Chinese, the primary reason for their willingness to work tends to be not wages/salaries or bonuses, but finding the desired guanxi circles. They are willing to do others favors as long as they feel that they have been accepted by the guanxi circle, that the guanxi circle, as a whole, is flourishing and promising, and that internal benefits are evenly shared. That's because they know that they ultimately will share more of the benefits as the guanxi circle develops. This is how they develop a sense of belonging to a small circle. On the other hand, however, Chinese will feel disappointed and leave an organization if they can never find the desired guanxi circle or if they join the wrong circle in which the leader fails to evenly distribute benefits or to allow for favor exchanges. Accordingly, a good leader is often able to manage a guanxi circle with the principles of family ethic so that all the members have a sense of belonging while seeing a growing number of resources available for operations. As a result, there will be more opportunities for achieving a win-win situation in future cooperation.

Sociologist He Cai saw a phenomenon of "inversely differential mode of association" while he was studying migrant workers in China's building industry. Cai finds that a contractor will first pay off overdue wages to jobbers or short-term employees rather than the long-term team members, when the contractor suffers a shortage of funds for a contracted project. At this moment, members of his guanxi circle receive worse treatment than that received by those outside the guanxi circle. This suggests that circle members of can work together to address challenges and do not care about short-term inequity. Instead, they care more about possible benefits from long-term favor exchanges. Notwithstanding, guanxi contracts with circle members will become invalid once they fail to receive the desired long-term benefits. In this situation, it is often very difficult for the ties to restore, and they may even lead to negative feelings.

Westerners typically believe that Chinese are collectivistic. This is because Chinese do show behavior characteristic of collectivism on many occasions and on a short-term basis. Accordingly, westerners are prone to reach a conclusion, through questionnaire-based surveys, that Chinese are inclined to be collectivistic. In the case of favor exchanges between pseudo-family and familiar ties, in particular, they are more often characterized by collectivism – prioritize the others' interests over one's own; owe achievements to all the people; help others without explicitly asking for rewards; always share benefits with others. Such seemingly collectivistic behavior, however, is intended, in the long run, to build up relations and ultimately achieve one's personal goal.

Carrying out favor exchanges to join a guanxi circle, therefore, is a major motive for Chinese to work.

5.4.2 Motive 2 – Building Your Own Guanxi Circle

Chinese join a guanxi circle to build up relationships so as to achieve their personal goals, but they need to have their own teams to do achieve their goals. Another important motive for Chinese to work, therefore, is building their guanxi circles.

To establish their businesses, Chinese are willing to preserve quietly for one or two decades and keep carrying out favor exchanges. But they make all these efforts in exchange for the day when a lot of their circle members will follow them and many others will come to do them favors once they call for support. The very reason for their receiving support at a critical moment lies in that they have carried out a large number of favor exchanges before; those who come to do them favors are all repaying favor debts. Accordingly, Chinese do most jobs to exchange favors with each other. A great motive for Chinese to work, then, is turning acquaintance ties into friend ones and a single instance of cooperation into long-term guanxi contracts through favor exchanges. These contracts will ultimately constitute a guanxi circle around someone.

Small companies tend to be the most energetic organizations in China and they all present a network-like structure. As an example, a very capable man leads ten capable ones, each of which in turn leads five less capable ones, each of which, again, leads ten employees. In reality, a structure of small guanxi circles embedded in a big circle is very efficient in China.

Chinese has a sufficiently strong motive to work and become most efficient only when they are given opportunities for organizing their own guanxi circles. Chinese workers will, therefore, seek a sense of belonging in the "big family", or their leader's guanxi circle, while seeking a sense of personal achievement in their own "small family", or the team that they build for themselves. They will always search opportunities for establishing guanxi contacts, or building up relationships, in order to be able to mobilize enough resources when needed.

If a worker can never establish long-term favor-exchange relationships with his or her leader and colleagues, he or she is always regarded as an outsider, then the incentives for him or her to work are nothing related to long-term, expressive ties. With the lack of encouragement by the sense of belonging, of the accumulation of relationships, and of opportunities for personal self-realization and achievement, such employees are much more likely to resign.

5.4.3 Motive 3 – Enfeoffment

A Chinese person of course will have a sense of belonging if he is admitted into a guanxi circle and given chances to exchange favors. But the best incentive indeed is letting him become an independent team leader, known as being enfeoffed in Chinese history: Let him be in charge of a particular field and lead his own guanxi circle to expand outside the organization. In principle, the team leader is required to submit part of his fruits to the mother organization, on the one hand, and is allowed to retain most of them and evenly distribute them among the team members, on the other, so as for him to build his own "family" and further organize a group of people to realize his personal goal. Self-organization is the very personal achievement that Chinese workers want most to make, and also is the most powerful incentive for them.

Likewise, while realizing his personal goal, the leader should establish long-term favor-exchange relationships with team members so that they will have a sense of belonging, more opportunities for building up relationships and equal access to the common pool resources of the team. And they may ultimately be given chances to organize guanxi circles for themselves and become independent leaders in particular businesses, so as to realize their personal goals. A successful leader will also effectively coordinate the goals of the "big family" and the "small family" and balance their interests. On the one hand, he will encourage the team members by letting them become independent team leaders. On the other, he will manage to let the "small family" continue working for the goal of the "big family." The guanxi circle theory emphasizes, therefore, that in China, the most powerful incentive is enfeoffment. A Chinese are good at finding a sense of belonging within the "big family" (i.e., his or her leader's circle) and a sense of achievement within the "small family" (i.e., his or her own circle). A leader who understands the Chinese way of thinking should make good use of the enfeoffment system.

5.5 Assumptions of the Guanxi Circle Theory

Based on the aforementioned characteristic analysis of Chinese behavior, we can see that the guanxi circle theory is built upon the following assumptions about humanity:

(1) The motive for people to work may carry out favor exchanges, so they will voluntarily perform tasks, or may want to evade responsibility. This depends upon who their exchange partners are;

(2) If the exchange partners are their familiar ties or members of their guanxi circles, work means favor exchanges and will be done by them on a voluntary basis; but if those who deliver work are acquaintance ties or people outside their guanxi circles, work is nothing but responsibility;

(3) Most people can only satisfy their need for self-realization by building their own egocentric guanxi networks and mobilizing the collective power of these networks. Accordingly, building up egocentric guanxi network through favor exchanges is an important motive for them to work;

(4) Most people, if they are able to establish favor-exchange relationships with the leader or a group of people, will form a guanxi circle, have a sense of belonging, work very hard, and, when addressing serious problems, be able to fully use their imagination, wisdom and creativity;

(5) Chinese employees who seek a sense of personal achievement will want to build their own teams and organize the team members to pursue their personal goals of life;

(6) A powerful motive for Chinese to work is giving them opportunities for self-organization and enfeoffing them so that they have a particular business that belongs to them.

With such assumptions about the nature of Chinese, the guanxi circle theory proposes an organizational model that is also situation determinism –i.e. core members, circle members and outsiders are identified in various situations, so that they will be treated by different principles of social exchanges..

Now that Chinese are good at favor exchanges and prone to form guanxi circles, there are always small or large guanxi circles within a Chinese-style organization that overlap each other. A successful leader will make good use of these guanxi circles by letting them organize into independent teams and contracting a particular business or being in charge of business in a particular place. By so doing, he will enable these groups of employees, who have a sense of belonging and a strong motive to work, to unleash their potentials freely.

By contrast, a failed leader is unable to control the development of guanxi circles and, hence, leads to a large number of closed cliques within the organization. Cliques become increasingly cohesive and decreasingly interactive with each other, and that will not mind sacrificing the interests of others for their own. This will usually result in fierce fighting among cliques, whose members rely on the collective power to work against policies and instructions from higher levels.

5.6 Dynamic Balancing of Guanxi Circles

5.6.1 Dynamic Balancing of Changes in Guanxi Circles

Given the aforementioned favor-exchange operations, we can see that familiar ties come with limited constraints and benefits, unlike family ties, including real- and pseudo-family ties, within a circle core characterized by unlimited responsibility, unbreakable ties and a closed group of core members. The existence of this buffer enables a guanxi circle to stay elastic.

An elastic operating mechanism has three advantages. First of all, it reduces structural constraints for ordinary members of the guanxi circle. Operations among familiar ties within the guanxi circle are rather elastic, as opposed to family ties within the circle core that stay loyal, that assume unlimited responsibility and that share all the secured benefits. Circle members will join collective actions when necessary, before sharing the fruits of these actions. Notwithstanding, their responsibility and favor exchanges are limited, so they also may not, if unnecessary, join these actions.

The existence of this buffer facilitates the resolution of the "tightly coupling" dilemma put forward by Granovetter (1995). Like most of the small groups, a guanxi circle is faced with a dilemma – it is ego-centered social capital (Lin, 2001) and the primary approach to mobilizing resources, on the one hand, and is faced with structural constraints (Burt, 1992) and a large amount of favor debts that dissipate resources, on the other. An entrepreneur has an important function that coupling social networks (Granovetter, 2002) to make them produce social capital, on the one hand, and decoupling them to avoid excessive structural constraints and needs for resources, on the other. Accordingly, how to balance coupling and decoupling becomes an important capability of an entrepreneur, and Chinese are always known for this (Granovetter, 1995). This is why Chinese are globally renowned for entrepreneurship.

As was proposed by Granovetter (2002), large social networks fall under three types of structures – highly decoupled, weakly coupled and highly coupled. The highly decoupled structure is full of guanxi circles with no bridge among them at all. The highly coupled structure is a high-density network that is unable to solve the aforementioned dilemma caused by tightly coupling. The weakly coupled structure is the only one with guanxi circles among which there are bridges. Once he is able to mobilize these guanxi circles, the leader will initiate large-scale collective actions in a large network. Good balancing will generate a weakly coupled structure, where the leader can take guanxi circles as the solid foundations for resource mobilization while maintaining the possibility of initiating larger-scale collective actions.

Secondly, the focal person of a guanxi circle may access resources from friends at critical moments, but may return at convenient times, the favor debts in a way needed by them at value much lower than that he or she originally received. This is just like a rotating credit association, where its head may mobilize huge amounts of resources at proper times but will reward the helpers at much later times. From the short-term perspective, delays in the rewarding can help the head get decoupled from excessive demands for reward in the high-density network.

The last but the most important point is: A guanxi circle has non-fixed boundaries. The phenomenon of guanxi circles is rooted in the Chinese concept of family. A Chinese person is always inclined to expand family ethics to social life beyond his or her family; a guanxi circle assumes some family functions for Chinese at work and life. This is why Liang Shuming (Liang, 1982; 1983) referred to Chinese society as "society based on family ethics." Yang Guoshu (Yang, 1993) put forward the concept of "family-orientation" – that is, non-family members can be socialized into a family and develop very close ties with it (Chua, et. al., 2008; Chua, et. al., 2009).

Like dynamic guanxi changes explained in Lecture 4, it is an important part of the Chinese culture to bring valuable exchange relationships into a guanxi circle from acquaintance ties outside it and to turn these acquaintances into good friends. Familiar ties constitute the primary cornerstone of ego-centered social networks in China. Most Chinese are inclined to dynamically move their relationships into and out of the three types of ties. Accordingly, a valuable and trustworthy acquaintance can be brought into a guanxi circle of friends to become its member.

In addition, identification with some roles can make a friend enter the core of the focal person's guanxi circle – family ties. In Chinese society, the identities of parties to a relationship are changed by means of marriage, adoption, becoming blood brothers, etc., to turn the ties between them into pseudo-family ones (Chen, 1994; 1995). People regarded as outsiders in western societies may find it easier, in Chinese society, to enter the innermost ring – family ties – through a new identity (Chen 1994; Luo 2005). Since such ties are not confined to family members, it is also called pseudo-family ties (Chen, 1994; Luo, 2005).

Chinese will see similarities to get to know more people, as is shown in the figure 4.1. The Chinese saying – "A maternal relative may be as distant to you as a stranger" – reflects the efforts by Chinese to seek similarities. Next, they will exhibit trustworthy behavior during exchanges with acquaintances, then carry out favor exchanges to establish long-term familiar ties and, ultimately, creating new identification with roles to establish family ties. These are part of the daily work and life of a Chinese person. A guanxi circle may be open, therefore, to acquaintances. Since every acquaintance is likely to become a friend in the future, obeying the principle of reciprocity is helpful for expanding the guanxi circle for the focal person. Likewise, the core of a guanxi circle, although tight and relatively closed, is not fully closed, making it possible for friends to join the Ban-Di(i.e., the primary, loyal team members and devoted followers, as we have explained above) of the focal person. Familiar ties blur the boundaries of a guanxi circle so that it can accept new members from the outside, on the one hand, and make the core team somewhat open to members other than those of the core team, on the other. This will leave more structural room for elastic operations during coupling and decoupling.

It is through this process that a Chinese person will know who in his or her social network can be mobilized to access what kind of resources. A person with good interpersonal relationships will mobilize the members of his or her guanxi circle to realize his or her goal. Also, he or she doubtlessly needs to help the members realize their respective goals during exchanges. How to maintain mutual trust within the guanxi circle tends to be the primary concern of Chinese at work. The elasticity of a guanxi circle – entry and exit are both allowed – decides that it is not closed; two guanxi circles may overlap each other and the overlapped part may serve as the bridge between them, plus considerable freedom.

5.6.2 Dynamic Balancing of Interests Inside and Outside Guanxi Circles

When in a guanxi circle, Chinese do pay more attention to affection and social norms than to short-term personal benefits and believe that relationships are essentially affective rather than personal benefits. This idea is doubtlessly a principle of family ethics. And it also is the outcome of the long-term strategy – building an ego-centered social network – in China. A person will face very high uncertainties by joining a long-term or even lifetime favor exchange. In this situation, doing fewer rational calculations and obeying norms will be a very good policy. As a Chinese proverb goes, "Doing others favors means leaving room for you." Chinese people may or may not follow collectivism, which depends upon the situation (Hsu, 1963; 1983). As for short-term exchanges within a guanxi circle, they are collectivistic in order to maintain harmony and create possibilities of future exchanges. From the long-term perspective, however, they will not necessarily sacrifice their personal goals for that of the group.

Accordingly, the "Yin and Yang" thinking also exists in operations inside and outside a guanxi circle. In a short period of time, some members of a guanxi circle act in a collectivistic manner, but this is, from the long-term perspective, only a process of achieving their personal goals. An actor exhibits loyalty in return for long-term social exchanges and this may also win trust from others, thereby expanding his or her ego-centered social network. From the long-term perspective, he or she can build his or her own guanxi circle to achieve a personal goal. Developing an ego-centered network and building one's own guanxi circle are among the most important motives for an actor to work.

As a result, exchanging favors becomes one of the major motives for Chinese to work.

Happiness at work, therefore, depends upon who is going to assign jobs. In other words, it is relationships – in addition to joy from work itself, loyalty to the organization and financial rewards – that encourage a Chinese person to work. Work is pleasant if it is about exchanging favors with the members of the actor's guanxi circle, because it helps him or her build up resources for his or her ego-centered social network. Otherwise, work is no more than responsibility if it is assigned by a person outside the actor's guanxi circle.

The focal person of a guanxi circle needs to regularly review the motives of the guanxi circle members. While enjoying their loyalty, team spirit and additional services, an excellent focal person knows how to encourage the members – that is, allowing them to build their respective small guanxi circles. In other words, the leader lets capable members build their respective guanxi circles, authorize these guanxi circles and grant them the power to make decisions. The focal person of the guanxi circle knows what the motives of the members are and will give them a hand at a particular time in the process of their accumulating their respective social capital. Once such a tacit agreement on long-term exchanges is destroyed, the feelings of mutual reliance and identification with the group (i.e., both parties to the relationship regards the other as part of their respective ego-centered social network) will disappear (Shen, 2007).

As a result, the phenomenon of guanxi circles has brought a fragmented structure to Chinese organizations, each of which may be divided into several guanxi circles, which in turn may each comprise a number of small guanxi circles. Chinese will really act with collectivism only when their personal goals are consistent with that of the organization. Unfortunately, such a group of people may form a trust network and can be defined as a group of actors who will interact and work only with people inside the network, a tight network built upon strong trust (Cook 2004; Cook et. al. 2004). We sometimes refer to such a closed guanxi circle as a "clique" – it loses connections with the other guanxi circles as a result of excessive tightness inside. Setting a unified goal within such a fragmented group poses a huge challenge for the leader of the organization.

On the other hand, however, the leader of an organization needs to equally distribute among all the subordinates within the organization, whenever possible, the resources that he or she owns, just like the principle of "equal sharing" within a "family" put forward by Zhai Xuewei (Zhai, 2001, 2005). But the leader also has his or her own guanxi circle, so he or she needs to maintain family-like ties with the guanxi circle members. The leader of an organization, therefore, should have a sense of responsibility for a larger network, such as the social network within the organization, while being able to build his or her guanxi circle to realize the personal goal. The principle of equal sharing for the larger social network, on the one side, and the principle of mutual benefit for the members of the guanxi circle, on the other, forms a second "Yin and Yang" dilemma.

An actor will build his or her guanxi circle to become a focal person, but he/she also will join the guanxi circle of the leader of the organization. For his/her part, the leader's guanxi circle is a "big family", while his or her own guanxi circle, where he/she is the focal person, is a "small family." The actor has senses of belonging and being safe in the "big family" while being able to rely on the "small family" to realize his/her personal goal. How can he or she behave in the "big family" such that he/she shows awareness of the collective interests while being able to secure resources necessary for favor exchanges in his/her small family? This is a big challenge for an individual.

To fight for resources outside the guanxi circle, the guanxi circle members generally will set a common goal to conduct collective actions. Such a guanxi circle can work for increasing the members' common interests. The focal person of the guanxi circle will rely on the joint efforts by the entire guanxi circle to secure more resources from a larger network, before distributing them among all the members to return their favors. If the focal person is also the head of the larger network, such as the leader of an organization, then he or she should play a paternalistic role (Farh and Cheng, 2000). In this case, the principle of equal sharing also applies to the larger network. This causes a role conflict. How can the leader of an organization maintain balance between favor exchanges within his or her guanxi circle and equal sharing within the larger network? This is a huge challenge for the leader.

In other words, the focal person of a guanxi circle is always faced with a universalism vs. particularism dilemma. On the one side, he is outside the guanxi circle, as he is the leader of the organization and the entire corporate staff expects that he regards the company as a "family", where resources are always equally shared. On the other side, he is inside the guanxi circle, where he needs to get emotionally close to the guanxi circle members by making favor exchanges, following particularism and favoring these members. Corporate employees outside the guanxi circle will complain if he fails to balance between the interests of his guanxi circle and the company, makes excessive favor exchanges and seldom conducts equal sharing. On the other side, the members of his guanxi circle will ask "Why should I be loyal and devoted?" and become increasingly disloyal if the leader always equally distributes resources and benefits and fails to favor his guanxi circle members. Likewise, this leader should follow the principle of equal sharing for all the guanxi circle members, but he has a core team within the guanxi circle, for which he should obey particularism. This constitutes another dilemma.

The interests of the guanxi circle members sometimes will be sacrificed as a result of the principle of equal sharing in the larger network. This phenomenon has been seen in a survey on China's building industry, where wages of the guanxi circle members may be paid later than usual while those of people outside the guanxi circle will be paid on time (Cai and Jia, 2009). A successful leader can always well balance the principles of favor and equal sharing, thereby enabling him or her to maintain harmony between his or her guanxi circle and the larger network (Zhai, 2005).

To sum up, a guanxi circle is in an ego-centered structure characterized by the differential mode of association. Accordingly, a circle has a core, inner ring of loyal, unbreakable and close ties. By comparison, the members in the outer ring are mostly those with whom the focal person of the circle carries out long-term, limited favor exchanges.

In the dynamic process, a circle may take outsiders into it or move trustworthy members in the outer ring into the core. In other words, the boundaries between the circle and the outside are blurred. In addition, a circle needs to dynamically balance expressive and instrumental ties to maintain harmony within it; it is also necessary to balance interests inside and outside the circle to maintain harmony with the larger network.

Accordingly, the aforementioned descriptions of circles lead to four conclusions – people inside a circle differ from those outside it; primary, loyal members differ from ordinary circle members; members in the overlap between two circles differ from the other circle members; teams that include power holders as the core differ from those without such powerful leaders.

5.7 Guanxi Circles and Flexibility

The phenomenon of guanxi circles can well explain why Chinese are flexible and changeable.

The Chinese culture is believed to be collectivistic and have a profound impact on the behavior within organizations, according to most cross-cultural management studies (Hofestede, 1980; Earley 1994; Chen, Chen and Meindl 1998; Morris and Peng 1994). Such positions focus on the closure of groups in the Chinese culture. If this were true, then Chinese organizations would not be that flexible and changeable; and Chinese, that entrepreneurial. Nonetheless, the ego-centered network of a Chinese person is found to be full of structural holes, and the Chinese himself or herself is good at discovering opportunities and starting up businesses. The *IMD World Competitiveness Yearbook* always list Chinese regions – Taiwan and Hong Kong – as the most entrepreneurial regions. And the entrepreneurial statistics well supports this finding.[1]

Why are Chinese good at discovering business opportunities? This is because their networks are also open. This can be proven by the phenomenon of guanxi circles, whose boundaries are relatively open and adjustable. There indeed are members in the outer ring of a guanxi circle who

---

[1] Ranking data was from IMD World Competitiveness Yearbook, http://www.imd.org/research/publications/wcy/index.cfm.

are identifiable from its core members, according to my EDA. Instead of being loyal and closed, ties between the focal person of the guanxi circle and the members in its outer ring are built upon long-term benefits and favor exchanges. These members, therefore, form a buffer that enables flexible guanxi operations. Among them, the bridges even have higher scores of job satisfaction, organizational trust and OCB than the core members who are at a relatively central position in terms of expressive ties.

Most Chinese sociologists also believe that Chinese are not collectivistic. Francis L. K. Hsu (Hsu, 1963), for example, explained the Chinese culture with the situation determinism theory. Liang Shuming (Liang, 1982; 1983) referred to Chinese society as "society based on family ethics." Following this thought, psychologist Hwang, Kwang-Kuo (Hwang, 2001) and Ho, D. Y. F. (Ho, 1993) referred to Chinese as "relationalists" to emphasize that Chinese society was relation-oriented. All these contentions highlight the importance of small, family-like egocentric guanxi networks in China. Why are there such arguments between these theories and the collectivism-centric contentions? The phenomenon of guanxi circles in Chinese society may provide an answer.

Under supervision with the powerful norms, all the guanxi circle members take collective actions for the group's interests and also, and indirectly, for their long-term individual interests. As Francis L. K. Hsu put it, Chinese behave in a collectivistic manner depending on the situation. Specifically, they behave in this manner only when the workplace is like a "pseudo-family." When relationships are potential lifetime ones and helpful for the future, the calculation of short-term benefits tends to be criticized as "foolish" while long-term investment in cooperative relationships is regarded as "wise." This has led to the long-term benefits-oriented Chinese thinking (Leung and Bond, 1989) and, accordingly, calculative people are usually unwelcome in Chinese society. Obeying rules to maintain one's reputation and to realize the long-term personal goal is the behavior recognized at work in China.

Guanxi circles reflect the collectivistic side of Chinese from the perspectives of short-term behavior and static structure. Nonetheless, a guanxi circle is not only a collective, but also develops around a particular individual. As an important motive for them to work, therefore, Chinese tend to join somebody else's guanxi circle through favor exchanges, thereby sharing more resources and increasing opportunities for favor exchanges to build up relationships. From a short-term perspective, Chinese do behave like a collectivist. But from a long-term perspective, we can see that Chinese persons with an ambition and a longing for success do so often to accumulate potential social capital so as to build their own guanxi circles and, in the future, realize their personal goals. Briefly, they are not collectivists from a long-term perspective.

The operating mechanism for familiar ties can well explain the method for balancing the relationship between individuals and the collective. Firstly, familiar ties, when compared with family ties, are the extension of family ethics. In the differential mode of association, however, they operate in a more flexible and open manner than that of family ties.

Secondly, with the "Yin and Yang" thinking, Chinese have developed methods for addressing conflicts between instrumental and expressive motives. The favor rule is one of the critical factors for understanding the Chinese behavior at work. It results from a combination of family ethics and self-benefit calculation. It is through favor exchanges that Chinese accumulate social capital, which is often believed to be more important than human and financial capital. These exchanges have therefore effectively increased the enthusiasm of Chinese, who then support the group's goal in favor exchanges so as to strengthen their trust-based relationships with its focal person. A guanxi circle emerges from favor exchanges among people who are in a relatively closed group and who have close ties with each other.

Thirdly, the "Yin and Yang" thinking also applies to balancing particularity and universality. To maintain the feeling of being identified within a guanxi circle, its focal person often carries out favor exchanges with his/her members. To increase harmony and trust between an ego-centered social network and the larger network, however, a leader needs to maintain the principle of equal sharing at work. The larger the ego-centered social network of the leader, the more successful his/her business. Nonetheless, he/she may have to face dissatisfaction within his/her guanxi circle. Maintaining harmony within the larger network usually will conflict with maintaining the interests of the guanxi circle.

The long-term benefits-oriented thinking emphasizes the particularity of familiar ties. When exchanges in a rather long-term manner are included, the calculation of short-term self-benefits is unable to avoid all risks. In contrast, obeying the norms will help a person maintain his/her reputation in his/her ego-centered social network. In a long process of dynamic balancing, the successful operation of favor exchanges enables a Chinese actor to avoid immediate conflicts between his/her guanxi circle and the larger network, on the one hand, and to leave room for initiating collective actions in the larger network in the future. Successful dynamic balancing brings a resizable, or elastic, scope of mobilized resources.

With familiar ties being the buffer, Chinese have resizable guanxi circles that can include acquaintances so as to access more resources available for mobilization when needed, and that, at other times, can become smaller to save resources and avoid excessive structural constraints.

Favor exchanges with familiar ties also maintain the elasticity of a guanxi circle, whose focal person can mobilize massive resources of all the members when necessary to finish a job. By comparison, the focal person can return these favors in other, and less costly, manners when he/she feels comfortable. Such delayed exchanges of heterogeneous resources allow the focal person of the guanxi circle to be very flexible in terms of mobilization.

Fourthly and lastly, familiar ties differ from family members (including real and pseudo ones) in that they assume only limited responsibility, together with interruptible favor exchanges and ties that are not so close that they should not be broken. Accordingly, the focal person of a guanxi circle can identify   circle members to participate in an action as needed and share the resulting fruits with them. The situation would be different in the case of Ban-Zi, as particular members form a symbiosis for which sharing is required for every action and, hence, the freedom of selection is unavailable.

The changeability of guanxi circle sizes, of the time to return favors, and of members who can be mobilized for an action enables Chinese to stay flexible and changeable in actions.

Lecture 6 Self-organization as a Mode of Governance

"...in The Book of Songs[1] it is said: 'He makes no show of his moral worth, yet all the princes follow in his steps.' Hence the moral man by living a life of simple truth and earnestness alone can help to bring peace and order in the world. In The Book of Songs it is said: 'I will keep in mind the fine moral qualities which make no great noise or show.' Confucius remarked, 'Among the means for the regeneration of mankind, those made with noise and show, are of the least importance.' ... 'The workings of almighty God have neither sound nor smell. There is nothing higher than that.'"

—The Doctrine of Dynamic Balance

Do Chinese have an indigenous set of management theories? It is necessary to see a fact before answering this question. Chinese enterprises indeed are very great – a phenomenon that should never be overlooked – despite so many problems with Chinese organizations as we have discussed above.

It is true and necessary that a large number of Chinese enterprises are taking their European or American counterparts as templates from which they learn modern management methods. But we have also seen that Chinese enterprises have already defeated a lot of companies from other countries in numerous fields, especially in the manufacturing sector. A student of mine studied one of such cases. She investigated a village that specializes in producing chain blocks. Products made by businesses run by local villagers have been sold worldwide and represent 70% of the domestic market. The second case is the China Commodity City (often shorted as CCC), a large wholesale market of Yiwu, a city in Zhejiang Province. Today, there are about 30,000 foreigners who make regular purchases in Yiwu, which is by far the world leader in terms of particular consumer goods. The third case is "no-brand-name" mobile phones (most makers of such mobile phones are small but actually not copying others' products and, instead, have their respective brands and R&D departments). "No-brand-name" mobile phones with advanced features such as dual cards, writing pad and high-speed camera are priced only somewhere between 600 and 700 yuan, as opposed to similar products from international brands priced at up to three times as high. Chinese-made "no-brand-name" mobile phones have been exported to many regions such as India and South America, where they are important competitors for products from major brands. Why are "no-brand-name" mobile phones so competitive? This is because makers of

---

[1] This is one of the main six books editted by Confucius. It is also translated as the Book of Poetry.

"no-brand-name" mobile phones are able to launch about a thousand models a year to meet the needs from niches ranging from senior citizens, children and migrant workers to white-collar workers. In reality, Chinese can usually provide very good products unless they are short of technological expertise.

How then have Chinese enterprises made all this happen? This indeed results from particular organizational structures. Why are Chinese enterprises so great in some organization structures such as the "one town, one industry" model in Yiwu, the outsourcing service network model in the construction industry and the field of high-tech manufacturing services, as well as the platform model of Alibaba and MediaTek (the latter provides technology platforms for the "no-brand-name" mobile phone industry)? And why are large companies such as state-owned companies, conglomerates and monopolized firms in China often the synonyms of inefficiency, hierarchy and wastage? These are the questions we should think about.

6.1 Explanations from Local Sociologists

I pointed out directly in the Preface that self-organization is the key to explaining Chinese managerial wisdom.

In China, the most advocated traditional managerial philosophy is "The best leader is the leader who does nothing against nature" (or simply, "do-nothing leadership"). When explaining the politics of do-nothing leadership in his book *From the Soil: the Foundations of Chinese Society*, Fei Xiaotong noted that there were three types of powers – dictatorial, consensual and educational powers. In the context of this book, China was a nation where dirt farmers constituted the majority, plus a large population and a relative shortage of farmland. As a result, Chinese farmers generally had small surpluses in addition to necessities of life; and China wanted not slaves but land when it expanded, so dictatorial power was seldom exercised in politics to seize slaves. Nor did China have the democratic tradition like in the West, so consensual power was not often used either. Given a large population, a relative shortage of farmland, small surpluses and dirt farmers as the majority, Chinese politicians mostly adopted a policy of letting the people live and work with high freedom.   It would take long for leaders to appear with superior capacities, ambitions and willingness to wage wars with other countries, such as Emperors Shihuang （BC.259-210）of Qin Dynasty, Wudi (BC. 156-87) of Han Dynasty and Taizong (AD. 599-649) of Tang Dynasty. If a ruler failed to recognize this and, instead, wanted to accumulate wealth and resources at a faster than normal rate, and attempted to do things overambitious and unrealistic, then he would often take the risk of enraging the people and result in a dynasty as short-lived as the ones founded by Emperors Shihuang （BC.259-210） of Qin Dynasty and Yangdi (AD.569-618) of Sui Dynasty.

The policy of letting the people live and work with high freedom emphasized the balance between the powers of the emperor and the gentry. In this context, the emperor's power represents the top-down central power of control; and the gentry's power, the bottom-up local power of self-organization. The latter power was manifested, after the Song Dynasty (AD. 960-1279), in self-organized units dominated by local clans, or a type of groups formed spontaneously on the basis of geography and blood relations. This led to a characteristic of the traditional Chinese politics – the emperor's power has no effect on the countryside – as there was no authority directly under the central power in places at levels lower than counties, which, instead, were basically governed by local clans.

The political wisdom of do-nothing leadership has translated into a tradition of self-organization by Chinese, whose capacity of self-organization, in turn, makes the politics of do-nothing leadership possible.

Fei Xiaotong believed that for rural society and self-governance by clans, the most important thing was not the dictatorial or consensual power but the educational power. The foundations for do-nothing leadership were, therefore, that this educational power was supported by the emperor's power and that the political leader doubled as a main participant in education in order to show his support for the family ethical norms in clan-based community. And this is why there was a tradition of "The emperor doubles as an educator" in China.

6.2 What is Self-organization?

Relative to self-organization is hierarchy, which refers to that a power holder controls a group of people and organizes them to finish an assigned task. By comparison, self-organization means that a group of people come together on a voluntary basis or as a result of inseparable relations among each other. It has the following characteristics:

(1) A group of people come together voluntarily on the basis of social relationships and trust;

(2) The group needs collective actions;

(3) The group sets formal and informal rules for itself in order to manage collective actions.

This concept is usually replaced by the term "network" in management studies. This term refers to that a group of small, self-organized units will form a network-like structure when combining into an entire value chain. The term "community" is usually used in sociology; and I refer to it as "self-organization", a term used by Ostrom (1990).

The concept of "self-organization" came from not social sciences but thermodynamics. Ilya Prigogine (Prigogine, 1955) first put forward this concept when he was researching the dissipative structure of systems. Later on, Hermann Haken (Haken, 1983) also worked on relevant issues when he studied the laser theory and founded synergetics. And research on self-organization has since made great progress in fields such as organic evolution, ecology and cerebral neurology. The Santa Fe Institute (SFI), which was co-founded by three Nobel laureates – Kenneth Arrow, Philip Anderson and Murray Gell-Mann, focuses on researching complex systems, especially the phenomenon of self-organization.

And the phenomena of self-organization and network-like structure also appear in the social and economic sectors. Physicists Duncan Watts and Steven Strogatz (Watts and Strogatz, 1998) used to research why frogs/glow-worms could finally synchronize their croaking/glowing at night. After fruitless contemplation, Watts thought, all of a sudden, of the experiment made by Stanley Milgram and found out that the interaction network of frog croaking was very similar with the interpersonal interaction network in that both of them were what Milgram referred to as a "small world with six degrees of separation." They published the result on the *Nature* as the most prestigious science journal (Watts and Strogatz, 1998) and the *American Journal of Sociology* (Watts, 1999), triggering a wave of research on complex networks in the field of social sciences.

What Granovetter（1995）referred to as "under-socialized" is like steam in which every free molecule moves randomly in the space and may interact with any other molecule that it meets. On the other hand, "over-socialized" is like ice in which all the kinetic energy has disappeared; in this state, individuals without activity only have very limited freedom and are faced with omnipresent restrictions caused by the field forces. The real world keeps changing between these states and, more often than not, we are restricted by the field forces on the one hand and are active on the other. More importantly, we can form groups, that is, self-organize into some fixed structures.

The concept of "self-organization" originally referred to a dynamic process in which a system evolves into orderliness from disorderliness. In the studies of governance mechanisms, the concept "self-organization" is always accompanied with "self-governance" put forward by Elinor Ostrom (Ostrom, 1990). With "self-organization," this book refers to a governance mode that differs from market and hierarchy. Instead of "network" used in management to refer to the structure of this organizational model, and of "community" used in social sciences to refer to a group of people who come together on the basis of affective and identity factors, this book uses "self-organization" to refer to the governance mechanism for this organizational model.

Although the concept "self-organization" was not first put forward by Chinese, the phenomenon of self-organization is at the very core of organizational issues and managerial behavior in China. A Chinese organization is always full of various independent units, such as entities operating under the name of the organization, business units that are contracted out, independent teams, and internal startups. Outside the organization are full of strategic alliances, business groups, outsourcing service networks, industrial cluster and small-firm networks. Why then is it like this? The common phenomenon of self-organization actually derives from the traditional Chinese way of thinking.

Chinese generally prefer being a leader in a small organization to being led in a big one. We may refer to it as the smallholder's thinking – that is, people always hope to have a "fief," i.e. an independent team or a business unit, which belongs to them. This is the most important motive for them to work. Before having such a "fief," therefore, Chinese may work hard by joining others' circles, doing others favors and building up their own relationships (or social capital). They can even wait for twenty years as long as they can have a team that belongs to them. And smart leaders also know when to recognize the employees' right for being in charge of a particular business field. In other words, they must allow their employees to lead their respective teams, or the latter ones will become decreasingly loyal. Given this thinking, energetic, independent, small teams are prone to appear in Chinese organizations. And there are interconnections within and between these small teams to form a network-like structure.

It is necessary to point out that to research managerial issues in China, we should first recognize the nationality of China. Today, there are always management researchers in China who want to neglect the cultural DNA of Chinese. Instead of leveraging this nationality and developing management methods to its advantage, these researchers always hope to isolate them from Chinese traditions before managing them with western methods of management. Speaking of relationships, they will think of making deals through the back door and giving bribes and will not be happy unless these relationships are removed. But this is impossible.

Firstly, relationships are still omnipresent and very influential in western organizations. Granovetter stressed that it was impossible to completely snuff out relationships. If social relationships and personal trust were snuffed out, then the transaction costs would become extremely high and business operation and management extremely difficult, because of the lack of basic trust. Secondly, if guanxi operation was completely snuffed out, then its advantages such as adaptability, flexibility and responsiveness would vanish.

Instead of simply regarding self-organization and guanxi as bad things, we should always pay equal attention to both sides of them, according to Chinese wisdom that Yin and Yang coexist and complement each other. It is true that fighting among closed cliques caused by guanxi circles as well as privileges and the back door resulting from manipulating guanxi are not good, but we should think about how to maximize the advantages of both and minimize their harms rather than reject them just because of their harms. In reality, every management system has two sides – its weaknesses will become obvious after its strengths are leveraged.

We should therefore first recognize the existing characteristics of Chinese society and Chinese persons' unquenchable longing for self-organization, before studying how to leverage its strengths and circumvent its weaknesses to realize the managerial philosophy of "do-noting-against-nature leadership" and "loosening control without causing chaos." Otherwise, Chinese employees will form closed cliques, fight with each other within the organization, and create a whole set of tacit rules to work against the formal regulations, if their longing for self-organization is always checked, and if they are never given opportunities for developing and making decisions independently in a particular field. How to use the right way to guide guanxi circle development and self-organization processes is the main maladies of Chinese organizational management.

6.3 The Relevant Theories in the West— Self-Organization as the Third Governance Mode

What we often refer to as "modern management", which is different from "traditional Chinese management", actually refers to a set of managerial theories and ideas developed in western countries and pioneered by Henri Fayol, Max Weber and Frederick Winslow Taylor. It is characterized primarily by hierarchy and scientific management.

6.3.1 The Principles of Hierarchy-based Governance

Max Weber elaborated on hierarchy as a governance mode, also known as bureaucracy, and summarized its characteristics as follows:

(1) There is clear division of work within the organization, where every member has clearly-defined rights and obligations;

(2) There are positions at multiple levels in a bureaucratic organization, where people are directed by their superiors;

(3) It is specialties that determine whether members of the organization are eligible for particular jobs or not; and there are clear, standardized procedures for every job;

(4) Managers are full-time functionaries rather than business owners; and they are not private ones and cannot work for private objectives;

(5) There are stringent, generally applicable regulations, rules and processes;

(6) Positions are independent of specific individuals; members have nothing among them but

working relationships, not to mention personal affection; the relationship between the organization and its members are restricted and protected by provisions;

(7) All the work processes are documented and archived.

For sure, these principles are designed for an ideal-type model. Modern management aims to design a large system and employ various means for hierarchical management, before ultimately realizing efficient collaboration within the organization. Such a system does have advantages over that of traditional organizations. Notwithstanding, it also have great weaknesses since it relies excessively on process designs, regulations and formal organizational structure. A lot of management scholars have long been aware of this problem and criticized hierarchy. Charles Perrow (1986) compiled, in his book *Complex Organizations: A Critical Essay*, the critical theories and pointed out that there are at least four major problems with hierarchy:

Firstly, stringent regulations result in a lack of flexibility within bureaucratic organizations, where excessive levels and processes are prone to cause slow response and inefficiency. When the external environment is changing rapidly, in particular, bureaucratic organizations find it more difficult to make quick adjustments, are short of innovations and, hence, find it difficult to adapt to the changes.

Secondly, hierarchy takes employees as screws on machines while overlooking their emotions and various needs. Such a practice limits the freedom of employees, makes it difficult for them to obtain a feeling of self-realization at work and ultimately reduces their initiative, spontaneity and creativity.

Thirdly, bureaucratic organizations are accompanied by huge powers. Employees in such organizations only execute directives from their superiors and this ultimately brings about a situation where huge powers are held by a very small number of officials. Process designs, regulations and formal institutions can only regulate repetitive jobs at low levels. With regard to decision making, the decision makers must be given enough freedom. As a result, the leaders of a small number of large organizations control massive resources but are seldom restricted by the principles of hierarchy. In this situation, the abuse of powers by the top management will cause extremely severe consequences.

Fourthly, such abuse of powers is most often manifested by the appointment of nobody but one's relations and the use of powers for private gains; decision makers who hold huge powers and are free from supervision will occupy the organization's resources, legally or illegally, or use them for private benefits.

Many western scholars after Weber have realized problems with hierarchy and proposed remedies from various angles, such as "The Functions of the Executive" from Chester Barnard, the human relations school of management, bounded rationality, the neo-institutional school, social network school and many other managerial thoughts. These thoughts propose various human-oriented management ideas and practices to correct restrictions and harms caused by hierarchy and scientific management to humanity, thereby encouraging employees.

6.3.2 The Embeddedness Theory of Granovetter

Governance structure is always an important issue in organizational research. Most of the previous research, however, explored how to select between market and hierarchy as two governance modes. According to the transaction-cost school represented by Williamson, for example, the dynamic effects of humanity and the transaction environment in the process of transactions cause market failure, difficulties in market transactions and extremely high transaction costs. The relative transaction costs constitute an important factor for determining the form of governance structure. Williamson takes network as a hybrid form of market and hierarchy. A subsequent series of studies all refer to network as a type of intermediate organizations while overlooking the existence of a third governance mode characterized by self-organization.

Nonetheless, Granovetter noted that Williamson's theory fails to notice an important thing – the trust-based relationships in economic actions. He said in his famous embeddedness theory that all economic actions are embedded in social networks. On the one hand, basic trust is required for any transaction, because no economic action can occur without it. On the other hand, trust is an important factor for deciding transaction costs and will change the selection of governance structure.

First of all, trust is a must and can never be replaced by institutions. I refer to this as the issue of "minimal trust." Although institutional design can reduce uncertainties and transaction costs, transactions can occur only when there is minimal trust between relevant trading parties. In an environment where nothing is trustable, nobody dare make transactions however perfectly designed the institutions are. For example, a Chinese person in an Africa country may even have no confidence in such transactions as renting a hotel room for a few days and, instead, must rely on the travel agency to transact for him/her. Doubts about local laws and the honesty of businesspersons in a totally strange culture will make it difficult for Chinese visitors to transact for themselves, even if they have signed contracts with the hotels and there are local laws that protect such contracts.

Secondly, trust-based relationships can replace institutions to a certain extent. Opportunistic tendencies and bounded rationality of people will result in higher transaction costs. Nonetheless, mutual trust between people, in addition to institutional constraints, can reduce these costs. Excessive contracts, lawyers and cumbersome supervision/examinations become less necessary if there are goodwill and high trust between both parties to a transaction. In addition, even if either party is found, in a post-transaction supervisory action, to have violated the contract, the other party will less likely file an immediate lawsuit for resolution. Instead, he/she probably will remain benevolent and settle the matter through private negotiations – that is, replacing the high lawyer fees with goodwill, whenever possible, so as to reduce the transaction costs.

Granovetter's analysis has shifted people's attention to social relationships and personal trust from the cold institutions, regulations and cost calculation. Since trust is indispensable on the one hand and can replace institutions and thus affect governance structure on the other, people should not rely solely on regulations and institutions in the process of management, but also value the effects of trust and relationships. In other words, they should balance between the "hard" institutions and the "soft" trust.

6.3.3 Woody Powell Regards Self-organization as the Third Governance Mode

In his article *"Neither Market Nor Hierarchy: Network Forms of Organization"* (1990), Woody Powell also criticized Williamson's position. He believed that self-organization (Powell used "network" instead, talking about the organizational structure rather than the organizational process) was not simply an intermediate structure between markets and hierarchies, but contained some special governance mechanisms – a governance mode built upon trust-based relationships.

He began to take networks as the third governance mode in addition to markets and hierarchies. All these three modes can be taken as the ideal types of governance structure, which in reality is always the hybrid form of the three. In this governance structure, trust-based relationships are built upon the perception that the parties to these relationships need each other, and can never be built upon authority-based or buyer-seller relationships. Trust-based relationships create a transactional environment that is mutually beneficial and open but not bureaucratic and restrictive (e.g., hierarchical) or free but doubtful (e.g. market). He then explained the differences among the three governance structures using the following table.

Table 6.1 The Modes of Governance—Taking Economic Organizations as an Example (cited from Powell, 1990)

	Forms of Economic Organization		
Key features	Market	Hierarchy	Network[①]
Normative Basis	Contracts-- Property rights	Employment relationship	Complementary strengths
Means of Communication	Prices	Routines	Relational
Methods of Conflict Resolution	Haggling—Resort to courts for enforcement	Administrative fiats-- Supervision	Norm of Reciprocity--Reputation concerns
Degree of Flexibility	High	Low	Medium
Amount of Commitment among parties	Low	Medium to high	Medium to high
Tone or Climate	Precision and /or Suspicion	Formal, Bureaucratic	Open-ended, Mutual benefits
Actor Preference or Choices	Independent	Dependent	Interdependent

With regard to formal rules, the main governance mechanisms under market structure include information dissemination, prices and contracts; those under hierarchical structure include bureaucratic structure, instruction system and organizational regulations; and those under network-like structure include trust-based relationships and negotiation, according to Powell. Network is not, therefore, a hybrid form of market and hierarchy or a transitional form between market and hierarchy. Instead, it is another governance structure with trust-based relationships at the core.

This position is supported by a large number of real-world managerial examples in China. Outsourcing by Chinese, for example, is a paradigm of governance based on the logic of network. But the most extreme case is what Perrow referred to as "small-firm networks" (SFNs). SFNs in China, especially in Taiwan, the city of Wenzhou, and Yi-Wu, etc., are often believed to be the best examples. In Taiwan, for example, some SFNs form a network with a core, but some others

---

① The governance mode of self-organization is generally called "network" in organizational sociology, since it has a network-like structure.

have no hierarchical structure, and the latter ones are represented by Wufenpu, the largest clothing market in Taipei. A group of small firms partner with each other, without the need for written contracts in a permanent network of suppliers. They needn't make inquiries or bargain like most other market players do; no firm is a focal entity to whose rules other firms are subject. Since every workshop is likely to become an outsourcer, no formal structure exists, let alone any formal instruction system. Since the corresponding governance structure mainly consists of negotiations and benevolent cooperation built upon trust-based relationships, not many written contracts, and no standardized business processes and instruction system, are needed.

6.4 Forms of Self-organized Units in China

What then are the forms of self-organization in Chinese enterprises? They mainly include independent units operating under the name of the enterprise, internal contracting, outsourcing and, as is also often in western companies, self-directed team and internal startup. In addition, if an enterprise does not know how to encourage its employees through enfeoffment, then it is prone to have closed cliques inside. A lot of Chinese enterprises are actually identical to modern organizations when it comes to the forms of self-organization, such as self-directed teams, profit centers, internal startups, outsourcing service providers and franchises. But there are two forms characteristic of China, as is described below. And there are some differences in the process of self-organization and the governance mechanism, for which I will try to make comparison in Lecture 8.

6.4.1 Operating in the Name of Another

An independent organization operating in the name of another refers to an organization that is independent of the latter, that operates in the name of the latter, but that maintains its independent organizational structure. In Chinese, this practice is called "Gua-Kao". Common forms of such organizations included university-run firms and collective businesses. A lot of university-run businesses were founded by the university's alumni and alumnae, who then partnered with their Alma Mater and ran the businesses in its name. These nominal branches of the university were actually independent organizations. Such organizations come into being for two main reasons.

The first reason is resources, including monopolized resources, brands and channels. A business sometimes must operate in the name of some other organization to access certain resources. Minerals or land, for example, is always controlled by the government or a few companies with concessions. To access such resources, therefore, some organizations opt to operate in the name of some other organization. The aforementioned school-run businesses fell under the category of relying on the university's reputation.

The second reason is legality, a factor highlighted by the new institutionalism. Legality is so-called wearing a "red hat" – when it comes to certain things, a company may meet with legality problems if it does them alone, but it can avoid this risk if it operates in the name of some other organization. One such example is the One Foundation, which was founded by Jet Li. This foundation once operated in the name of the Red Cross Society of China because it is very difficult for an ordinary organization to become eligible, under the current system in China, for raising charitable funds from the public; only a few large foundations have this right. The One Foundation has no choice, therefore, but to operate under the Red Cross Society of China, or its fund-raising activities would become illegal.

It would be easier for us to understand, from the perspective of new institutionalism, the phenomenon that a large number of companies operating in the name of another emerged in the 1980s. It was in that period of time that the ban on the private economy was just lifted and founding private businesses remained on the verge of being legal. A large number of private companies therefore opted to operate in the name of another and appeared as collective businesses. But later on, there were still many private businesses that opted to operate in this way even though they had become legal ones. They did this for rationality: the past experiences had caused a stereotype that the state-owned economy was the only safe and trustworthy one, and that private companies were dishonest. Accordingly, operating in the name of a state-owned enterprise, especially a central one, would be prone to leave an impression that this company was very good and strong.

An issue that worth research is: Does the phenomenon of operating in the name of another also exist in the West? Franchises in the West are actually very similar with Chinese organizations operating in the name of another. Franchises themselves of course come in different forms. Such companies as the KFC have more controls over their franchises. In addition to paying for franchise fees, the KFC franchises are required to purchase foods from the designated suppliers, decorate the restaurants in a unified manner and carry out standardized staff training. By comparison, some other franchises face no more requirements than the code of conduct and the sharing of incomes on a pro-rata basis. These franchises are very similar with Chinese organization operating in the name of another. And this is a very interesting managerial phenomenon and organizational issue. In reality, the western franchise system has had numerous Chinese characteristics since it was introduced into China. Financial regulation over a lot of franchises, for example, has gradually become less tight and evolved into a form that resembles "paying tribute." What exactly, then, are the differences between franchise and operating in the name of another? How big are the differences between these two systems? Both of them deserve in-depth research by scholars.

Another example is 7-Eleven convenience stores in Taiwan, where the company had two systems. Stores run directly by the company were named 7-Eleven, while those simply operating in its name were named "PECOS." The stores of both types belonged to Uni-President Enterprises Corporation (UPEC), but all the stores of the latter type have been shut down while the ones of the former type are still operating. This indeed is a very interesting phenomenon. What exactly are the industry environments more suitable for branch stores than Gua-Kao? These issues also deserve research.

6.4.2 Internal Contracting

The second phenomenon of self-organization in China is internal contracting, which occurs in two forms – business contracting and product contracting.

We have talked about DoubleStar that declined as a result of family-tie breakup. It relied on self-organization in the early growth stage and exemplified the old Chinese saying that "Loosened control leads to prosperity." The predecessor of DoubleStar was a state-owned rubber factory, which was on the verge of bankruptcy and was therefore forced to turn to some other business. After it began making sports shoes, however, it was struggling since it was unable to catch up with Chinese-made products of international brands in terms of quality and brand. In this situation, the DoubleStar chairman, Wang Hai decided to contract provincial businesses to excellent employees, with a hope that they could rely on their respective capabilities to develop the local markets.

In 1998, Wang Hai initiated, among all the local branches, a reform based on the internal contractor system. The reform was characterized by: Private buyout plus the exit of state-owned capital; and each contractor and agent should repay by year the discounted fund that it owed the group. And it turned out that "Loosened control leads to prosperity" – DoubleStar achieved success with its internal contracting strategy. Although they were defeated by competing products from international brands in Tier 1 cities, DoubleStar sports shoes were very popular in Tiers 2 and 3 cities, especially in southwestern China. DoubleStar had built, around 2008, a dozen of low-cost production facilities in mountainous areas in the provinces of Shandong, Henan, Sichuan and Guizhou; and it had deployed a marketing network of ten business areas, over 200 agents and over 5,000 chain stores represented the ones in southwestern China as well as the provinces of Shandong and Hebei. DoubleStar sports shoes took the first place among competing products in terms of sales revenue for ten consecutive years, making it a well-established leader in the Chinese Mainland's shoe industry.

Wang Hai had two regional managers as his major assistants and candidates for future promotions within the DoubleStar Group. They even became Wang Hai's nominal son and daughter. And they were Liu Shuli and Han Junzhi, a couple. This internal contractor in southwestern China was finally reformed into Chengdu Technology Investment & Development Co., Ltd. ("DoubleStar Southwestern China"), a private company co-owned by individual shareholders led by Liu Shuli. DoubleStar Southwestern China rose at an amazing rate under the contractor system based on power and profit sharing. By the end of 2007, DoubleStar Southwestern China had seen total assets of nearly 3 billion yuan, net assets of 1.5 billion yuan, and annual sales revenue of 7.5 billion yuan. It had nearly 2,000 specialty stores (including stores operated directly by DoubleStar and franchises) across southwestern China. By comparison, DoubleStar Group had only about 5,000 specialty stores across China. At this moment, DoubleStar Southwestern China was more than a contractor and agent, as it had a shoe and clothes production capacity that even exceeded that of the headquarters. Moreover, it had controlled most channels of DoubleStar. DoubleStar Southwestern China was actually sharing the DoubleStar brand with the DoubleStar Group. In 2008, DoubleStar Southwestern China represented 50% of the total sales volume of the group. Both the strong enthusiasm brought by internal contracting and family-like trust enabled DoubleStar Southwestern China to make extraordinary achievements.

The second form of internal contracting is product contracting. A rice seller, for example, may segment its products into several categories, for each of which a different person is responsible. Jack, again for example, may be responsible for selling ordinary rice; and Tom, for "healthy rice" that contains whole grains. And modern organizational management also includes institutions that resemble the internal contractor system, such as the cost center (or profit center) advocated by Peter Drucker, internal startups and self-directed team within the corporation. These institutions are all characterized by monitoring only results, no longer monitoring processes, minimizing intervention in personnel management, giving opportunities for making decisions and, lastly, assessing performance on the basis of results. And these institutions all come with power sharing to a high extent despite that they differ from each other in terms of how dividends and equities are distributed. How does internal contracting in China differ from these modern management institutions? This is another interesting issue in the field of organizational research.

6.4.3 Forms of Self-organized Units in Modern Management

In addition to the above-stated forms, today's Chinese firms also learn a lot from the similar practices of their Western counterparts. The concepts of "management by objectives" (MBO) and "cost center" were developed by Peter Drucker in the 1960s and 1970s when the so-called "knowledge workers" emerged. They were then valued and popularized by the business world. In a strict sense, they don't count as self-organization, because the MBO may target an individual rather than a team, and the units of a cost center are not necessarily formed by employees on a voluntary basis. Notwithstanding, these institutions recognize relevant organizations' rights for defining rules and processes and managing for themselves, and they base assessment only on the ultimate performance.

Internal startups or self-directed teams are the forms of self-organization that developed from modern organizational management. Internal startup "companies" or self-directed teams are entitled to define rules and processes and manage for themselves. Moreover, they have team members recruited on a voluntary basis, that is, the majority of the personnel-relevant power. But I still differentiate them from the Chinese-style internal contracting, because internal contracting sometime can be so structurally loose that it is hard to call it an institution. A group of employees, for example, can solicit business in the name of the company as long as they have paid the required deposit. Such a governance mechanism, which is built upon not formal regulations but relationships and trust, demonstrates one of China's qualities – it is "guanxi society" or "favor-exchange society."

Likewise, the phenomenon of operating in the name of another in China sometimes demonstrates the aforementioned quality, so it is somewhat different from franchises and chain stores in modern management institutions. The same phenomenon – what used to be an external independent organization is now operating in the name of another – is accompanied by more guanxi-based governance mechanism in China. This issue deserves in-depth research by management scholars in China.

The last and ultimate form of self-organization is outsourcing, that is, making the internal contractor an independent company and, during long-term transactions with it, regulating relationships with it through guanxi management and the transaction governance mechanisms.

Outsourcing may also cause problems, of course, especially when there are excessive levels of outsourcing plus ineffective control. Both the cave-in at a site of the Hangzhou subway construction project and the toppling of a building in the city of Shanghai resulted from blurred responsibility and utter ineffectiveness of regulation caused by excessive levels of outsourcing. Work outsourcing is omnipresent in China's construction industry. This suggests that China's construction industry is energetic and efficient. On the other hand, however, a lack of governance mechanisms, excessive levels of outsourcing and bad control often sometime result in quality problems. How to design a mechanism that allows outsourcing to serve as an incentive, on the one hand, and realize the scenario of "loosening control without causing chaos"? This question requires contemplation by managers.

6.4.4 Closed Cliques

A guanxi circle, if enfeoffed, can turn into a self-organized unit that relies on a group of people to develop in a particular field. If it is not well managed, however, the guanxi circle may evolve into a closed clique in the organization – particular persons form a small group where all the individual interests are tied with its success – and bring about mistrust and disagreement between its members and people outside it. The phenomenon of closed cliques marks a point at which the effects of relationships turn to negative from positive.

Cliques exist in almost all organizations, but strangely enough, management scholars have made little research on them. One of my students researched knowledge management and found out that acquiring tacit knowledge is an important reason for Chinese to join guanxi circles. This conclusion resembled that of research made by Granovetter, who found out that when exploring racial problems at work, it was difficult for African Americans to become competent for jobs that required higher skills, not because they had no sufficient professional capabilities, but because they were unable to enter small circles within the company and, hence, to acquire tacit knowledge. "It is the mentor who guides you into a field," as a Chinese saying goes, but the problem often is: No mentor is available. When it comes to a job, it is easier to master its technical part, but the most important part is tacit, such as: How to survive in an organization? What are the relationships between people in the organization? Who are the key members? What are the styles and preferences of the leader? What are the preferences of various customers/clients? What are the skills critical for the job? It is very difficult to write down these contents, which, then, can only be imparted by the mentor. In western societies, whites represent the majority of internal circles of persons who do higher-level jobs, but few of them are willing to mentor African Americans. Consequently, African Americans are unable to acquire important tacit knowledge and, hence, to obtain clues about their tasks, despite that they are excellent also. This tends to result in poor performance at work. In China, therefore, new employees typically hope to find and join the right guanxi circles rapidly so as to receive help, especially tacit knowledge, from circle members.

Closed cliques (or "Pai-Xi" in Chinese) in China are very distinctive and differ in many aspects from the ones in the West, despite that they are conceptually close to each other. As one of its characteristics, a clique in China generally is not only a congregation of a small number of people in an organization, but is also accompanied by the appearance of rules for self-management (i.e., tacit rules). Moreover, these rules will be used to negate the formal ones. It was for this reason that I sometime translated "Pai-Xi" into "gang". Another similar concept is "faction" in politics, but factions usually appear because of policy-orientation or ideological differences, as opposed to cliques that are strongly relationship-oriented.

6.5 Formation of Self-organized Units

Self-organized units are formed in two stages. Firstly, a number of people form a small group. Secondly, this small group also needs to have a particular common goal, for which division of work, cooperation and collective actions are carried out. The small group can be called a self-organized unit only after it has entered a phase of self-governance and spontaneously take actions for the same goal. Otherwise, it remains only a small group. Five or six familiar ties, for example, like gathering at their leisure and killing time by playing cards and chatting. By this moment, they have formed nothing but a small group. And this small group can be called a self-organized unit only when these persons have a common goal such as promoting environmental protection, assign tasks in a planned manner, carry out activities such as making open speeches and handing out leaflets in a sustained manner, and set rules for themselves.

The formation of self-organized units typically requires a process, and this process is the very sub-issues of our research on the dynamics of self-organization.

First, a number of people congregate and have a growing number of social network connections among each other, or increasingly strong interrelationships.

Then, a small group comes into being. With a growing number of internal connections, people in this small group become increasingly distant with the others in the larger organization. As for this stage, if we analyze the small group using the social network analysis method, we can see that the relationships among these people begin to become dense, and those between them and the outsiders, sparse. By this moment, they can be regarded as having formed a small group.

Latter, identification appears within the small group, where the people begin to have a clear understanding of the differences between them and the outsiders, and to become aware of their identity as a member.

One of the main reasons why Chinese are good at self-organization is that they know just how to create identification. Particular people without blood relations among each other, for example, may also find their common ancestors who lived several thousand years ago, and they may even jointly build an ancestral temple. Some other people, again for example, may find a common teacher so as to become schoolmates. And people may also become blood brothers, even if they can find no interrelationships, to create identification like that of the Gang of Thirteen Brothers (a guanxi circle in the Taiwanese congress).

Next, the small group defines a common goal and begins to take collective actions to realize this goal.

Finally, the group will also gradually develop internal formal and informal rules and a mechanism for collective supervision to assure that the common goal is smoothly realized.

What are the theoretical explanations for the popularity of self-organization as a governance mode in China? I propose some explanations as follows.

6.5.1 Grouping by Favor Exchanges -- Explanations from the Perspective of Network Dynamics

In Chinese society, favor exchanges constitute an important and special phenomenon. On one hand, favor exchanges are hidden under expressive ties, so neither a clear statement about rewards nor bargaining is allowed. On the other hand, both parties to such exchanges each have a favor account in mind. The favor giver will not talk explicitly about any future reward, while the receiver should not forget the favor and must record it into the favor account so as to return it in the future. Accordingly, the favor giver will first think of the receiver, when he/she needs help, and ask the latter for help; and the receiver will return the favor to show his/her sincerity of gratitude. Moreover, the receiver may return more than what he/she received and make the other party owe him/her a favor to ensure that their favor accounts can never be cleared off. Since both parties seek long-term ties rather than the fairness of every single transaction, the favor receiver will, when he/she needs further help, think of not only those to whom he/she did favors but also those from whom he/she received favors. It doesn't matter that more favors have been owed, because familiar ties can be enhanced as long as the favor debts are returned and the norms for favor returning obeyed on a long-term basis. It is in the process of giving, receiving and returning favors, once and again, that familiar ties are established and strengthened. The evolution and development of such ties will gradually lead to the phenomenon of grouping and, under particular circumstances, to the formation of guanxi circles in organizations.

So the very first step of research on self-organization is to ask: What are the relationships that make a group of people get closer and closer to each other? In my research on the phenomenon of self-organization in the village reconstruction after the Sichuan earthquake, I find that the local networks for mobilizing relationships were mostly built upon schoolmate, old friends, townsmen and pseudo-family relations. But a phenomenon unique to China is that there must be a focal capable man who acts as the leader during mobilization. Chinese call this focal person "capable man".

The key to the occurrence of self-organization in China as a guanxi society is not only that the community itself has basic social capital available for use, but also that there is one or a number of leading or elite citizens. These elite citizens will take on the leading roles out of consideration for social status, prestige, honor and responsibility for public trust, not only for   physical gains.

The phenomenon of capable men demonstrates what Fei Xiaotong referred to as ego-centered social networks with the differential mode of association; and capable men always begin mobilization in their respective social networks. The process of mobilization is often characterized by a capable man mobilizing a group of his followers, who in turn begin mobilization in their respective social networks. This is how a group gradually expands and shapes up in such a snowballing process.

The aforemenon networks built upon favor exchanges will gradually become permanent under certain circumstances and turn into small groups that always carry out exchanges inside. My students and I tried to simulate the process of favor exchanges between Chinese using a dynamic simulation model (Chang and Luo, 2007). It turned out that we reached some very interesting conclusions. Firstly, the phenomenon of grouping by favor exchange is prone to occur in an organization in the model when it is relatively short of, but not in bad need of, resources. When there are abundant resources, all the persons will more likely help each other generously and be less motivated to exchange favors with particular persons, making it more difficult to build a segmented social network. When resources are hardly available, the persons are inclined to do short-term exchanges, making it difficult to develop familiar ties based on long-term exchanges.

Secondly, the stability of resource distribution is a moderate variable for the effects of the amount of resources on the phenomenon of grouping. In other words, it is more likely for guanxi circles to appear if there is huge variance in the amount of distributed resources among individuals at times. By comparison, it is less likely for the phenomenon of grouping to occur if resources are distributed on a relatively even basis.

Thirdly, grouping will more likely occur when there are effects of "partnering with the rich," which refer to that people typically opt to exchange favors with those who are more popular and that it is easier for a person to establish relationships with more people if he/she has a better-developed social network. It is in this situation that the phenomenon of grouping is more likely to occur.

These are only hypotheses generated from the simulation model and have yet to be proven or disproven by real   data. Current social network analysis is able to identify static small groups, but the process of relationships evolving within small groups and that of their becoming permanent have yet to be further researched in the field of network dynamics.

6.5.2 Establishment of Identity – Explanations from Social Psychology

After a small group is formed, people in this group will have a feeling of identity. Finding a "flag" to identify with can justify the cohesion and exclusionism of people in this group while strengthening the ties among them.

Social psychologists have made much analysis of why people get together, before identifying two primary reasons: Identity and trust. Identity can be established upon numerous factors such as class, religion, region, status and team. And it can also be built upon non-inherent factors. Users of Apple computers, for example, may identify with each other because of the brand's effects – they feel themselves superior to ordinary PC users. Factors like this are created by a group of people.

When researching consumption in the cultural sector, Pierre Bourdieu noted in his book *La Distinction* (1984) that both education and culture are instruments for distinguish the inside from the outside and generating identity. Taste indeed comes from a complex social process and includes the exclusive occupation of particular social resources and knowledge. A person shows his/her temperament, education level and lifestyle through his/her cultural taste; and a group of people also differentiate themselves from others trough their unique taste. Since a social group conveys its cultural symbol – taste – to its members through socialization, taste will serve as a flag that marks the members' identity with each other when different groups are competing for social resources and even the dominant position. People can identify "friends" and "foes" rapidly with information revealed by consumer behavior. And taste can also be passed on to the next generation as an instrument for the class's self-reproduction.

Another important mental factor is trust. Karen Cook (Cook, 2004) found out, after studying the phenomenon of underground economy in the early stages of the Eastern Europe reform, that trust was an important condition for the operation of organizations involved in the underground economy. There was a high level of trust within these organizations, where a person could receive trust from the others and carry out transactions only after he/she became a member of the group. And that is often how regional business groups come into being in China. In the meantime, a group will use a complete set of internal tacit rules to resist pressure from the outside. The study made by Cook indicates that economic activities of a particular type will lead to a lot of small groups if they are illegal and can be carried out only when a high level of trust exists.

Identity and trust may appear before a small group is formed. Loose groups of Wenzhou-based businesses are built upon the regional factor; and there may be alma mater-based groups of industry professionals who graduated from Peking University and Tsinghua University respectively, for example. But a small group may also appear before its members seek a flag to identify with, such as a school, a corporate vision, a created myth or an ideology. In reality, Chinese are good at creating identity spontaneously organized group. Even clans in China are not necessarily based on blood relationship. As Sociology Professor Zhang Xiaojun notices, a lot of clans are spontaneously organized – a group of people with no blood relationship toward each other may also co-build an ancestral temple and self-organize into a kin.

A small group of people with strong interrelationships will take collective actions as soon as it sets a common goal. And a set of governance mechanisms is necessary for these collective actions to last and be well organized so as to realize the long-term goal. Self-organization leads to a third governance mode beyond market and hierarchy. And the last stage of building a self-organized unit is to establish a self-governance mechanism.

6.5.3 Behavioral Logic of Self-organization

The aforementioned three governance modes differ from each other not only in rules but also in internal membership, operating logic, and the nature of powers.

Hierarchy relies mainly on bureaucratic control, obedience and instruction system. Its members have a collective identity in it; the logic of power is followed; and powers are top-down. Hierarchy requires the building of a complete set of top-down bureaucratic systems, leading to higher managerial costs.

Self-organization relies mainly on voluntary cooperation among the members, whose in-group sense is based on expressive ties, common identity and shared memory; the logic of relations is followed; and powers are organized in a bottom-up manner. Relationships and trust are important factors for self-organization, so governance will generate guanxi costs for building and maintaining relationships.

Market relies on free competition. Players can freely choose trade partners in the market; the logic of contracts and transactions is followed; and powers are decentralized to every transaction participant. Market will generate transaction costs.

A lot of successful practices have emerged since self-organization as a governance mode appeared in the field of management. Peter Drucker took the lead by putting forward the concept of "cost center", before those of "self-directed team" and "internal startup" emerged, and was followed by other concepts such as authorization, empowerment and accountability.

For the part of Chinese, they are especially good at self-organization since it is a millennia-old tradition of the Chinese culture. They have thus developed a lot of good models, such as the "Little John Wayne" of the Fung Group and the managerial idea of "To make the dragon (i.e. the leader) dream come true, there should first be a group of dragons with no head (i.e. many small leaders who are independent from the leader)" created by Stan Shih, the founder of the Acer Group.

In China, the ancient managerial concept of "do-nothing leadership" is intended to create a good environment the governance of self-organization; and we have now seen a great deal of successful "experiments" in modern society. Why is self-organization-based governance ideal for the Chinese culture? How can it become successful? I will explain them in the next two chapters.

Lecture 7 Dynamic Balancing between Hierarchy and Self-organization

"Confucius said: "There was Great Shun[①]:-He indeed was greatly wise! Shun loved to question others, and to study their words, though they might be shallow. He concealed what was bad in them and displayed what was good. He snatched up the two extremes, determined the Mean, and employed it in his government of the people. It was by this that he was Great Shun!"

—The Doctrine of Dynamic Balance

Since most Chinese organizations have a bureaucracy, or hierarchy, to control a network of comparatively independent subunits, how to make balance of hierarchy and self-organizations has become the most interesting issue in the research of Chinese management. Thus, the most important thing for managing organizations under the doctrine of dynamic balance is balancing tightened and loosened control, that is, powers in hierarchy and the ones in self-organization.

7.1 Explanations from Local Sociologists

By putting forward "the emperor's and the gentry's powers," Fei Xiaotong was the first local sociologist to talk about how to balance the top-down hierarchical and the bottom-up self-organizational powers. On the one hand, the emperor's power went down to counties by appointing governors, who were members of the hierarchy. On the other hand, clans' power was exercised in a bottom-up manner; squires were the leaders of autonomous groups but were not members of the government hierarchy and not subordinated to the local county governors. These two powers were bridged by the county governors' subordinates, petty civil servants and, in clans, conciliators appointed by the local governments (this job title differed from place to place in China).

What conciliators did was a piece of drudgery, as the powers of local self-organized units were actually held by squires. Since squires did not deal directly with the local county governors, conciliators became the gatekeepers for the emperor's power to influence the countryside. Petty civil servants transmitted administrative orders to conciliators, who in turn executive these orders

---

[①] An ancient great Chinese emperor.

before submitting relevant reports to their superiors. A conciliator would be imprisoned if the local squire thought of an administrative order as being improper and decided to defy it. By this moment, the county governor would talk with the squire to reach a consensus and push for execution of the order. Their reputations were maintained as the conciliator would be punished for doing a poor job in executing the order. There were times when it was difficult to reach a consensus on executing an administrative order or when the local governor played politics in this process. In such a situation, the squire would mobilize relationships that he built up in the officialdom and relied on the government at a higher level to restrict the local governor. The squire therefore acted as a protector of the local self-organized unit.

If it was very difficult to execute an administrative order, the squire could ask a higher-ranking official, with whom he had a good relationship, to convey his opinion to the group of civil servants who stood for the Confucianism, which asserts the restriction of emperor's power. And if he had served as an official in the capital of the country, the squire could even directly ask a particular central government official to convey his opinion. In the meantime, he could rely on a protest by the clerisy and the Confucian orthodoxy to refute the administrative order as departing from local conditions and being arbitrary, or to report the improper execution by particular local officials that had caused great trouble to the local people. This led to dual management systems of the political organization in China. Specifically, political management in China did not rely solely on a rational system implemented in a top-down manner, as there were also effects from self-organized grass-roots groups built upon the use of power in a bottom-up manner and upon interpersonal relationships in clans. With the Confucian orthodoxy counterbalancing centralized governance to a certain extent, it was possible to let high-ranking officials in the bureaucracy know the needs of local self-organized units so that they could make decisions with these needs in mind.

The rapid development of local self-organized units also received acquiescence from the then Chinese government; administrative districts below county level were autonomous and social functions of clans were mostly respected by the government with exception to taxation, conscription and forced labor. Coordination by the clan was a mediation mechanism dominated by the clan's authority, based on its own internal rules and intended to maintain internal harmony. Every clan had the authority to discuss important internal affairs at the ancestral temple and to arbitrate internal disputes, and decisions reached by arbitration were binding upon relevant clan members. Chinese villages were always a part where it was more difficult for national laws to work. It was therefore impossible to rely solely on national laws to coordinate relationships and mediate disputes in rural communities. As a result, a considerable part of coordination and mediation was carried out within the clan.

In a "guanxi society", there are social networks connecting political elites on the top and the grass root gentries, and bridging ties thus help balancing the top-down and bottom-up powers in the ways that Fei Xiaotong illustrated. So the political organization in China was not a hierarchical one spanning level down to the grass roots, but -two levels with a hierarchy to control a network of comparatively independent entities. Specifically, there was a top-down hierarchy at the county and higher levels, while, at the grass-roots level, there were self-organized local autonomous entities controlled by squires who did not subordinated to the hierarchy. Fei Xiaotong referred to this system as "dual lane political systems." The clerisy acted as a bridge between the powers at the higher and grass-roots levels. On the one hand, they formed a group of civil servants to prevent powers of the hierarchy from overexpansion. On the other hand, they educated local people on norms and virtue behaviors rituals so as to maintain the order in self-organized units.

7.2 The Relevant Theories in the West--Rational Selection of Governance Mechanisms

When should a leader, of either an organization or a government, loosen control, that is, grant powers so that the people can form self-organized units? And when should the control be tightened, that is, strengthen hierarchy-based governance? There are two considerations: Under which circumstance it is suitable for loosened and tightened control respectively? Does excessively loose or tight control likely occur?

The 2009 Nobel Prize in economics were won by Oliver Williamson and Elinor Ostrom, both of whom specialize in governance theories. Williamson studies how external environment and transaction characteristics affect the selection of governance mechanisms, and he has argued that network is also a governance structure, which is the hybrid form of market and hierarchy.

According to Williamson's transaction cost theory (Williamson, 1985), transaction frequency, asset specificity and environmental/behavioral uncertainties will affect the selection of governance structures. When a transaction is highly asset-specified and faces uncertain environment, market-based governance does not apply since transaction costs are too high; and hierarchy-based governance should be employed instead to carry out the transaction inside the organization, as this will reduce environmental hazards and transaction costs. On the other hand, employing the market-based governance structure to obtain resources becomes more economical if all the three factors are low. Williamson first proposed network-based governance structure, such as strategic alliances and outsourcing, in his analysis, but it is only a transitional form between market and hierarchy.

Nonetheless, Powell (Powell, 1990) made it clear that network is not a hybrid form of hierarchy and market, but a third, and new governance mode. It has unique governance mechanisms, internal operating logic and rules, which are different from those of hierarchy or market.

Moreover, Granovetter noted in his embeddedness theory (Granovetter, 1985) that Williamson's analysis overlooked an important factor – real trust in economic transactions. Firstly, mistrust and infighting between employees actually represent a large part of managerial costs; and mistrust between the parties to a market transaction adds much to transaction costs. Interpersonal trust may greatly reduce managerial costs in an organization or transaction costs in a market and thus changes the selection of governance structures. By extending Granovetter's argument, hierarchy-based governance is not necessarily a good choice for replacing market, and that self-organization-based governance is the choice for minimizing transaction costs, when there is sufficient trust.

Secondly, minimum trust is indispensable in the process of any transaction. Otherwise, it is impossible to carry out transactions inside or between organizations however perfect their institutions are. Again by extending Granovetter's argument, there should be governance mechanism involved based on self-organization principles in any transaction, either in or between organizations.

On the basis of the aforementioned studies, trust can be taken as a key variable, which is the precondition for selecting a governance structure, into William's transaction cost model. When environmental uncertainty, hazards of measurement, asset specification and transaction frequency are high, the market-based governance will not be suitable any longer. If the required real trust in a transaction is high, then carrying out transactions by hierarchical mechanisms is not necessarily the preferred governance structure. In this situation, self-organization may be employed to reduce transaction costs through trust-based relationships and the negotiation mechanism.

On the basis of these theories as a whole, I may simply say that self-organization becomes the best governance option if the transaction of a particular "product" demands a high level of real trust between the two trading parties and if there indeed is sufficient trust to supply. To sum up, a transaction requires real trust between the two parties if it has characteristics as follows:

(1) Behavioral uncertainty is high, and it is difficult to use observable measurement tools to collect performance indicators, not to mention explain employees' performance using statistics;

(2) The product is highly differentiated and even on a one-to-one basis. This requires a lot of communication and is prone to cause information blockage or asymmetry. By letting a relatively

independent team deal directly with consumers, therefore, it is possible to make quick decisions, depending on the specific situation, to satisfy diversified needs;

(3) The product is about personal feeling. Again, it is difficult to measure performance using objective statistics, on the one hand, and massive information is required, so it is advisable to let a relatively independent team to deal directly with consumers;

(4) The product is cooperation-based. Specifically, cooperation between the supplier and consumers is required for the product to work, such as education, medical care and community security, because the feeling of trust between the two parties is crucial for the result of their cooperation;

(5) The environment is extremely uncertain, so flexibility, quick response, and a relatively independent team that is able to make decisions at any time are needed;

(6) There are no conflicts of interest between the two parties to the transaction. Some financial products on which bets are placed, for example, will damage trust;

(7) Information is highly asymmetrical. Lawyers, accountants and R&D staffs in the knowledge industry all have expertise that is hard for consumers to fully understand. And it is difficult for any transaction to occur without real trust.

Briefly, market-based governance does not apply to the "product" of a transaction if this product is accompanied by high behavioral/environmental uncertainties, asset specificity and transaction frequency, as was analyzed by Williamson (Williamson, 1996). But which should be employed in this situation, hierarchy- or self-organization-based governance? If this "product" meets the aforementioned conditions, then it requires very strong real trust. And if the parties to the transaction happen to trust each other, then self-organization-based governance becomes the best choice. Otherwise, rational transaction parties would prefer hierarchy-based governance.

Sufficient supply of real trust is the base for self-organization mode of governance. Chinese managerial wisdom, including purifying one's mind, cultivating one's characters, managing guanxi, building guanxi circles, and balancing Yin and Yang dynamically, is for maintaining strong real trust, so that it cultivates a good environment for self-organization-based governance.

7.3 Balancing among Market, Hierarchy and Self-organization

7.3.1 Extending Governance Modes to the Public Sectors

Selecting from among the three governance modes – hierarchy, market and self-organization – is necessary not only for a specific organization, but also for public administration. In this situation, hierarchy refers to reliance on the government's top-down powers, while self-organization refers to reliance on social forces, or various non-governmental voluntary organizations, such as NPOs, associations, clubs and communities. Accordingly, these three governance structures are also called "government", "society" and "market" respectively.

The same concept of "self-organization" has long been explained in numerous theories with respect to public governance. Next, I would like to use Nan Lin's theory (Lin, 2009) to explain sociological theories and positions on this issue. Most sociologists believe that three forces – government, market and society – should coexist in public governance. Public sectors can develop harmoniously only when the three forces are well balanced and work together. Lin referred to the three forces as "governmental power", "individual rights" and "community power." Among them, "governmental power" refers to the government's top-down hierarchy-based governance; individuals' rights, which mainly include property rights, refer to people's rights for free exchange in the marketplace; community power refers to the bottom-up power held by self-organized units.

There are a wide range of communities that lead to community power. Specifically, communities in our society include NGOs, clubs, online virtual groups, professional groups, industrial associations, urban communities, rural autonomous groups, etc. In the future, online virtual groups will become a more and more important form of self-organized unit in China. For example, travel mate clubs were such important communities during the donation process after the 2008 Sichuan Earthquake. These clubs consist of travel lovers who chat online and travel together when free. After the 2008 Sichuan Earthquake occurred, a large number of travel mate clubs organized their members to contribute to the post-quake reconstruction. They donated money or necessities, or spent their holidays participating in the reconstruction efforts in the quake-stricken areas. Such community actions were among the examples of community power.

Industrial associations are another type of communities. When I was having interviews with some managers in high-tech manufacturing, I was impressed by what they told me, "This community is just a small world with only a few hundred so-called players." It is for this reason that the insiders will always know who has done something bad or which company makes products of poor quality. Industrial associations therefore play the role of internal supervisors in the industry. Regional groups, such rural clans and urban apartment complexes or street committees, may also self-organize into associations valuable for property management in apartment complexes and for creating a better public life.

Ostrom was a pioneer in proposing self-organization as the third governance model in public administration; she took the management of common pool resources for example. When it comes to research on the governance of public resources, tragedy of the commons used to be a common issue. Since the ownership of common pool resources is unclear, people tend to use them from the perspective of maximizing personal gains, while overlooking the protection and long-term management of these resources. This typically results in damages to the resources. There are two traditional solutions to this problem – relying on the market or on the government. As for the first one, certain mechanisms are devised to make users pay for their use of public resources, or, alternatively, to privatize these resources. Nonetheless, full privatization is often infeasible in reality, and it is very difficult to devise perfect mechanisms. As for the second one, the government decides who has the right to use public resources such as land and mines, how to use them, how long they can be used, etc. One of the risks with this solution is that the power holder is prone to abuse the public power, which in turn causes defalcation, corruption and other malefactions. Ostrom found out, therefore, that in addition to government and market, there was the possibility of self-governing public resources: hierarchy-based governance applies to products that are publicly owned and publicly used; market-based governance applies to products that are privately owned and exclusively used; and self-organization-based governance (or self-governance) applies to products that are publicly owned and exclusively used.

7.3.2 Dynamic Balance in the Mind of Chinese

I have mentioned two important concepts above – what Fei Xiaotong referred to as "the emperor's power" and "the gentry's power." Balancing between these two powers, which represent the powers of the top-down hierarchy and of bottom-up self-organized units respectively, was the very pivot of Chinese politics, according to Fei. There indeed was a set of structures and mechanisms in the history of China that had undergone changes one after another over the past millennia, according to Ray Huang in his book *China: A Macro History*. And this mechanism actually dealt with balancing between the powers of the hierarchy and self-organized units. If they were poorly balanced and the central power was much weaker than bottom-up ones, then turmoil would likely occur, along with fragmentation among competing warlords. Or alternatively, if the central government maintained so tight control as to deprive all the regions of vigor and growth opportunities, then the whole society would likely go stagnant and finally lead to revolution. Realizing a balance between the powers of the hierarchy and self-organized units – that is, avoiding the scenarios of "Loosened control leads to prosperity" on the one hand and "Tightened control leads to recession" on the other – was crucial for the prosperity of every Chinese dynasty.

It is advisable to balance the powers of market, hierarchy and self-organized units, but one of the current existing problems in China is that we pay attention only to governmental and market power, that today's Chinese scholars are always arguing whether we should let the market be the arbiter or strengthen the government's regulation, but   society always plays an insignificant role.

The mainstream generally talks about only the government's regulation or market forces. Moreover, those who advocate market forces are inclined to attribute all the current social and economic problems to an underdeveloped market; and those who advocate the government's regulation, to a chaotic market, together with the opinion that the government's intervention is needed.

By comparison, Chinese followers of the doctrine of dynamic balance always believe that neither overdoing nor underdoing is good and that diverse things coexist, complement, compete with and stimulate each other – that is, there is dynamic balance among them. How then do we know when to loosen or tighten control?

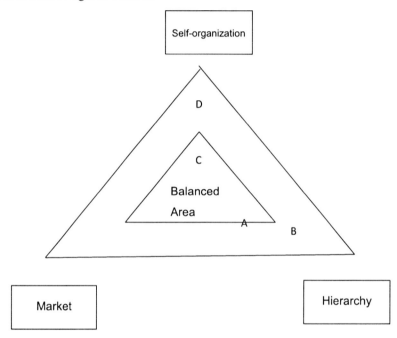

Figure 7.1 The Diagram of Balancing Governance Modes

Take the governance of a certain affair for example. If you have used the aforementioned analysis method and seen that neither market nor self-organization but hierarchy applies, then you should the governance combination at Point A (see the figure 7.1). In other words, the doctrine of dynamic balance will argue that good governance structure must allow for the coexistence of the three modes. It is a combination of various governance mechanisms, which include more or less the principles of each mode. Otherwise, if you go to an extreme and reach Point B, then you have left the balanced area and will immediately see weaknesses of hierarchy, including the over-centralization and abuse of powers, a system that is devitalized by too many formal rules and thus becomes stiff, etc.

Dynamic balance stresses that the situation varies with time. As an example, there has been higher trust between the parties to a transaction in the system, and the nature of the transaction has changed so that real trust is more needed than ever. Hierarchy-based governance therefore becomes unsuitable. It is necessary at this moment to move to Point C from Point A. But if you move too far and reach Point D, then you have gone to another extreme and will damage the system. You should then manage to move back to Point C from Point D so as to reenter the balanced area. This is dynamic adjustment, the way of seeking dynamic balance.

Confucian ethics and family ties constitute the traditional base for self-organized units in China, but, in modern society, self-organized units rely more on volunteerism and philanthropy to function. In reality, however, both Confucian ethics and family ties are having decreasing effects on Chinese society. Modern ideas from the west have been impacting on community forces for more than a hundred years. In addition, the growing market forces have caused great damages to community forces since China began reform and opening-up three decades ago. The market is damaging communities more severely than are any other forces. In rural communities, for example, capable people in the prime of life have all gone to work elsewhere, leaving the elderly, weak, female and children at home. Marketization and urbanization, together, have exhausted the resources of rural communities, which are therefore short of capable men and leave no one to conduct self-organization process. On the other hand, however, both volunteerism and philanthropy have yet to grow up in Chinese society, where the influences of morality and ethics needed by modern societies remain too weak and the number of self-organized units is still far from enough. The society will certainly become unbalanced if this situation continues. To realize harmony, Chinese society must value and foster the forces of self-organized units.

7.4 Managing Self-organized Units

The issue appearing immediately after self-organized units are created is how to manage them. This issue had long been neglected by economists till Ostrom won the Nobel Prize in economics. And studies about self-organization have since received increasing attention. Next, we will compare Chinese and western cases by taking particular self-organized units– industry associations for example. On the one hand, a Chinese organization always needs to manage self-organized units within it, such as internal contractors, independent subunits, self-directed teams, etc., and at the same time, it needs to deal with networks of firms outside the organization, such as business groups, subcontracting systems, local industrial clusters, etc… Firms in a local cluster often self-organize themselves into industrial associations. On the other hand, industrial associations are communal forces in the governance of public sectors. An industrial association is a good case for our study, since it is a bridge between organization-level and public-level governance.

7.4.1 A Chinese Case

There are more than 1,600 furniture makers in City L, Hebei Province, China, who sell products in all the municipalities and provinces as well as thirty-five oversea countries and regions such as the EU, the Middle East, Africa, Southeast Asia and Americas. In 2009, the city's furniture industry saw a total output of 10.5 billion yuan (RMB; about 1.7 billion U.S. dollar), 13.28% of which came from exports. When it comes to metallic and glass-made furniture, City L ranks the first across China in terms of production and sales volume, as it represents 65% of the total volume of such products in China.

(1) The Beginning of the Furniture Association

Before the furniture association was founded, there were already over 1,000 furniture makers that formed a full industry chain in City L. Nonetheless, there were still copying, price competition and poaching among these businesses.

At that time, furniture maker associations had already grown relatively mature in Guangdong Province, including the city of Shenzhen. The furniture exhibition held by Guangzhou Furniture Association (GZFA) had become very popular; Shenzhen Furniture Association (SZFA) also had opened an R&D center to promote technological innovations in local furniture industry. There was little communication among City L-based furniture makers that were then competing fiercely with each other; despite that they knew the above-mentioned developments and also hoped that there could be a similar organization to help them develop. It was said that "We all talk with each other in such a way as not to reveal any secret" and "It's even difficult to have dinner together. And we won't talk with each other since we are competitors", a furniture maker said. As a result, nobody was willing to start organizing.

In March 2004, City L's first ever furniture association was officially founded with support from the municipal government. But when they faced this newborn industry association for the very first time, most business owners felt strange and ill at ease despite the government's strong support. In an election organized by local economic committee, W, who was believed to be excellent and innovative, was appointed as the president. W was also running a furniture factory in City L, where he was known as a man who "dares to tempt fate" when it comes to investment and innovation. In addition, he was generally recognized in terms of morality and capacity. Unfortunately, the association did nothing but hold two meetings within the first year after it was founded. The attendees did negotiate about stopping forcing each other to cut prices, but to no avail. At last, the association looked as if it did not exist, and its members gradually quitted.

(2) The Appearance of a Capable Man

The local economic committee organized a second election for the furniture association on May 10, 2005. Among the four candidates, WHL (called President Wang hereinafter) was unanimously elected as the president. In addition, fifteen vice presidents were elected and they were all well-known furniture business owners in City L.

Unlike the other members of the association, President Wang of the new association specialized not in furniture manufacturing but in real estate operations. He was thirty years old in 2005 and was believed by other local entrepreneurs to be a "down-to-earth" young man with great achievements and good word of mouth. At that time, President Wang and his company were planning a commercial real estate project named the Furniture Exhibition Mall; he was responsible for building a new furniture market larger than the old one before renting or selling booths to City L-based furniture makers. "Everybody will receive many opportunities from this platform, including our own business opportunities," said President Wang when explaining why he joined the furniture association. He believed that City L's furniture industry was very promising, but distribution channels remained a weakness at that time. The old furniture mall, which was opened in 1993, could no longer satisfy the furniture makers' needs in terms of size and infrastructures, but a quick-witted President Wang perceived business opportunities from this problem. "The market comes first. We are thinking that to make a good market, we need to consolidate the furniture industry," he said. With the opportunity of planning the Furniture Exhibition Mall, President Wang as a layman joined the furniture association.

The second election, though so named, indeed was nearly equal to founding a new association. Apart from the original name, there were changes in everything ranging from members of the association and members of its board of directors to articles of association. After he was inducted into the association, President Wang first organized a team responsible for its work. He appointed Mr. Zhang, an excellent employee of his company (called Secretary Zhang hereinafter; he was later on appointed as the general manager of the Furniture Exhibition Mall project), as the secretary general of the association, for which he hired six full-time staff members.

(3) A Critical Mass – the Formation of the Core Team

Given the failure of the old association, a lot of former members were no longer willing to join the newly founded one. After President Wang was inducted, Secretary Zhang had the staff members visit more than 300 local furniture makers – they explained what was new about the association and invited the makers to join it. Fifty-four makers joined the new association shortly after it was founded; only a dozen of them were the former members of the old one. These 54 makers formed the initial "critical mass" of the new association.

Four months after it was founded, the new association successfully built a good image by organizing its members to participate in a Shanghai-based exhibition. It then began receiving the members' trust and support. For this exhibition, the member companies needed only to ship products and arranged them at the exhibition site, while the association was responsible for everything else, including decoration, booth arrangement, booth distribution (i.e., the exhibitors' relative positions), coordination with the host, etc. The association discussed with the twelve exhibiting companies about how to allocate the sizes and locations of the booths, before agreeing to follow the principle of equal sharing. After the end of the exhibition, the exhibiting companies from City L each received orders worth twenty to thirty million yuan. This success made the association much more reputable in the industry and allowed it to work more smoothly afterward.

According to the critical mass theory co-developed by Oliver and Marwell (1985), a critical mass refers to actors who advocate cooperation and who take lead in participating in it. They are critical for the realization of cooperation. For the part of City L-based furniture makers, they can receive returns in two aspects – operating in a competitive environment with good order and benefiting from the influence of local brands – for what they do for the furniture association (e.g., membership fees, time to attend meetings, self-restriction as required by the association, etc.). But neither return would be impossible if only a few companies were willing to join the association and obey the common norms in early period of cooperation. Expected benefits from the association can be realized only when a considerable number of companies are willing to cooperate, stop price competition and spend money on branding campaigns. Operation of the furniture association is therefore characterized by increasing marginal utility; inputs and initiative of the critical mass are crucial. The team led by President Wang and Secretary Zhang, plus the earliest members, became early and primary promoters of the association.

(4) Self-governance Mechanism

As members of the furniture association increases, how does the association regulate the industry in order to effectively monitor unfair competition among fellow member companies? As a self-organized unit, the furniture association has no power to forcibly regulate its members and have no formal regulations to monitor them. Its articles of association, which are fewer than 1,500 Chinese characters in length, specify nothing but broad definitions of its functions as well as the members' basic rights and obligations. Article 13 provides that the association's functions include "Coordinate to settle disputes in the industry and avoid unfair competition in it." Nonetheless, no article has further regulations on the members' behavior. As for the members' obligations, there are only three provisions: "Support resolutions passed at the members' meetings; keep the association's internal secrets; actively participate in its meetings and activities and improve your company's production and operations so as to contribute to the growth of this industry." There is no word about forbidding unfair competition, much less corresponding provisions with regard to penalties. The only job of the association that is directly related to unfair competition is assisting the local administration of technology supervision in amending local regulations. Moreover, the local administration of technology supervision is the one that publishes and implements these regulations, as the government has not granted the association the power of regulation. In fact, the secretary general of the association has confirmed that the association is only a coordinator and service provider, which advocates a good competitive order but will not regulate it through formal institutions. As the secretary of the association X_ZM put it:

"The association will not intervene in how the companies do business. We recommend that everybody stay away from poaching, price competition, reliance on low prices and inferior products, and unfair competition. We help people broaden their horizons so that they see what is happening elsewhere ... The association itself has no institutional requirements on any individual or organization."

"(The association) only provides a platform. You can leave if you don't want to be in the group. The guys were even unwilling to have dinner together, but now they have much better relationships with each other."

The furniture association prioritizes promotion of communication among the businesses. First of all, the association holds business salons twice a month so that the entrepreneurs get together, talk with each other and share experience in the tea party. Topics for the business salons differ from session to session and cover important issues that affect corporate growth, such as steel market developments, sales issues and booths at the exhibition mall, etc... Secondly, the association makes full use of formal meetings as the opportunities for communication, as it holds a vice-president meeting every two months, an executive-director meeting every six months, and a plenary session annually. These meetings are more than ceremonial, as they hold in-depth discussion among the members on major issues that affect industry growth. Lunches and dinners will also be available for the member companies to have more opportunities for separate communication. In addition, the furniture association conducts many other events such as exhibitions, purchaser meetings and training. While helping the member companies broaden their horizons and understand the markets elsewhere, the furniture association works to enhance informal communication among Town S-based businesses by means of dinners, etc. As the secretary general X_ZM said:

"Today, if certain persons of some other association come here, we will call particular business owners or executives and say that 'Would you like to join us this evening?' or 'Would

you like to talk with us?'"

The association encourages the local businesses to actively share experience. On the one hand, it encourages larger businesses to release new product designs on their own initiative. On the other, it persuades smaller ones to abandon malicious poaching and turn to learn from their larger counterparts.

"We tell the businesses that 'If you have any new ideas, just speak out. In this way, the other people will be ashamed to copy them. Otherwise, they will copy them instead.

"Every business indeed has been on the wrong path. And instead of poaching its people, it is advisable for you to avoiding taking such a wrong path. It has certainly paid a price for having been on the wrong path and you will also pay a price for poaching. In other words, learning from its lesson is better than poaching its people. In reality, these large businesses will not be stingy with their experience after you have a pleasant talk with them."

With all these efforts made by the association, there are increasing interactions among the entrepreneurs, who have become willing to trust one another and discuss business issues, and can even visit each other's businesses to learn the latter one's experience. The communication platform created by the association has led to increasing communication among City L-based furniture makers, as a growing number of them are willing to frankly share ideas. As a member of the association XG_Y said:

"There has been an obvious phenomenon of frank communication since around 2006, especially since 2007. After a sufficient number of communication activities were conducted by the furniture association, people have found out that fighting between each other is actually not a good thing."

Since the local furniture makers have a stronger identity with one another, a lot of entrepreneurs have become familiar ties who often have dinner together or talk with each other by phone. As a result of increasing communication between the entrepreneurs, an originally fragmented furniture industry has begun becoming a social network with strong interactions.

(5) Reputation Mechanism in structured social capital: Social Network as a Watchdog Mechanism

Significant changes in City L's furniture industry have taken place since 2006 despite the lack of formal regulations. There are now much fewer cases of poaching and copying. When asked about the reasons, the local entrepreneurs often mention a phrase – "feel ashamed." As a local entrepreneur YS_Z said:

"Today, we are very united and want to expand the business. This association gives us opportunities for communication with one another and, at least, there are fewer cases of poaching each other's employees. We all have a sense of shame and will feel ashamed (if we do a

wrong thing)."

Now that the furniture association as a communication platform was established and a social network of furniture makers built, norms have gradually come into being within the network and begun regulating its members. As was observed by Masahiko Aoki (Aoki, 2001) in Japanese villages, members of a social network will obey its norms once they feel the threat of being expelled and rejected – this threat as an informal but believable penalty will put the members under stress. "Feel ashamed" indeed acts as a negative-screening incentive, because an entrepreneur believes that he will be noticed and condemned by his peers if he has done any wrong such as poaching or copying. This potential stress caused by the peers' opinions will make the entrepreneur feel ashamed or even dare not face the other members of the network. If a company violates the rules of the network (e.g., by committing unfair competition), then it will be faced with not only the stress from the peers' opinions, but also real-world punishment. This is because "If you hurt me once, I will hurt you twice." Once it ignores the peers' opinions and condemnations and insists on committing unfair competition, the company will be jointly rejected by the others that have decided to "hurt you twice." Specific manifestations may include the company's being excluded from the circle of information sharing and discussion, no other company being willing to deal with it or share experience, and even other companies' possible retaliation in a similar way (e.g., by poaching the company's people). The watchdog role of a social network becomes more obvious in the following statement of the furniture association's general secretary X_ZM:

"The old association was nominal at best and was unable to often get people together. I might have heard about your factory, but I didn't know you and would not meet you. Then I would have someone poach your employees because I knew they were excellent and, anyway, we didn't know each other. But now, we get the business owners or executives together from time to time, so they have become familiar with each other. When they meet, they will greet each other by saying things like "So you are President Zhu" or "So you are President Wang. Your business is pretty good." And then they will talk to share experience. Now that they've known each other, they will of course scorn to poach each other's employees ... This is like the Beijing people in the old time who lived in Siheyuan (Chinese quadrangles, which literally means a courtyard surrounded by four buildings). We are all very familiar with each other, so things like clothes hung by any of us in the courtyard will never be lost."

Once a close social network is established, the pressure from negative screening in the network will urge its members to obey the informal rules and act to show good will toward each other. Under such supervision in the social network, companies will begin, when faced with competition, to show stronger willingness to cooperate. Moreover, communication and cooperation between the companies will also make their employees dare not leave a job at will. This is favorable for the stable operation of all the furniture makers, thereby benefiting them in the long run. Now that they have felt the benefits of cooperation with each other, the companies will become more willing to join the association and work actively with it. Another noteworthy phenomenon is that the constraints from "feeling ashamed" are effective only within this social network. Although they now no longer poach each other's employees or copy each other's products or ideas, City L-based companies still do so frequently to their competitors based in Guangdong or even foreign countries, as a member of the association HF_C said:

"We used to copy each other's products or ideas. But we have changed our mind since the association led us to see the outside world. We are now copying from the outside instead of copying each other. We have been brought to another level as we are now copying from Guangdong. And we are also copying from foreign competitors."

This also suggests that self-discipline of City L-based furniture makers, which are members of the association, results from the pressure that they feel in the social network within the association. Once they are outside the network, the negative-screening incentive created by the pressure from the peers' opinions will no longer exist and, naturally, the resulting supervision will also disappear.

7.4.2 The Case of Western Counterpart

Next, I will use an American case to discuss characteristics of rules set by Western self-organized units. Compare how the City L Steel & Wood Furniture Association ("the furniture association" stated above) in China and Semiconductor Manufacturing Technology (SEMATECH) operate, and we can get some interesting theoretical insights.

(1) Semiconductor Manufacturing Technology

Founded in 1987, SEMATECH was America's first ever large-scale, intra-industry R&D consortium and is believed to be a paradigm of cooperation organizations. Given its initiative and huge influence, American scholars have made in-depth research on how it was established, together with detailed records of its history (Browning and Shetler, 2000).

In the 1970s, a crisis was sweeping the then fragmented U.S. semiconductor industry as a result of fierce competition with Japan. It was in this context that SEMATECH was formed by fourteen members, including Intel, IBM and AT&T, which were all high-tech leaders in the semiconductor industry and combined to represent 85% of the U.S. semiconductor market. They are the critical mass of this association, and jointly established SEMATECH as equal partners. Its staffing mechanism was noteworthy during the formation of this consortium.

SEMATECH has staff members in two categories: Assignees from its member companies and full-time employees. The assignees typically work for two years, after which they will mostly return to their companies and continue with their jobs. These people generally are middle or senior managers or technologists, who, as senior industry professionals, have superior professional and managerial capabilities and thus are able to assure that the consortium can promote industry growth. While working at the consortium, they may also be still working at their companies and, during the operation of the consortium, protecting the latter ones' interests. On the other hand, the full-time employees specialize in organizational work of the consortium, make sure that it operates in a sustained and stable manner, and act as third-party coordinators during conferences to promote discussion and communication among the companies.

The assignees in SEMATECH provide a variety of professional skills and industrial judgments for the consortium to make decisions, while the full-time employees enable it to maintain a relatively impartial position when it is necessary to coordinate interests of all relevant parties. Particularly important are SEMATECH provisions concerning the president's qualifications: The president shall not be an assignee from a company and must cut off all the business ties with his/her original company to work on a full-time basis.

If the president is from one of the fourteen SEMATECH members, which have equal rights and obligations, the other members will feel that their interests are threatened. As a result, the president can receive trust from all the member companies only when he/she is not from any of these companies and plays a third-party role. The first elected president of SEMATECH was Robert Noyce, a co-founder of Intel who was then a member of its board of directors. And he resigned from Intel, as required, after he was elected as the president of SEMATECH.

The founders of SEMATECH were aware, at the very beginning, of the importance of creating a trust mechanism. Given a fragmented industry, Noyce received trust from all the member companies thanks to his third-party status, despite that the election of president was made more difficult by the provision that the president shall be a person from outside the member companies (some executives with rich experience and superior qualifications are unwilling to abandon their positions in their respective companies and, hence, to serve as the president). As was said by Charlie Sporck, a co-founder of SEMATECH, this is an important precondition for SEMATECH to develop smoothly without the threat of breaking up owing to disagreement on interests.

(2) The Code of Conduct

Shortly after they founded SEMATECH, the founders developed specific regulations with regard to various matters and compiled them into a book. This four-inch-thick book details the consortium's future main tasks, work plans, behavior, etc. The code of conduct is divided into four parts: Organizational framework, funding, personnel arrangements and government relationships. And each section consists of numerous, more specific issues, including Total

Quality and other sections. This book was drafted by several persons in charge before it was submitted to a plenary session for discussion. There were heated debates among the assignees who were racing to recommend modifications to both provisions and details on behalf of their respective companies. To be able to gather all the members' opinions, the plenary session and debates lasted for two days before an agreement on the main provisions was reached. These provisions detailed all relevant parties' rights and obligations, and the members gained a clear picture of the consortium's main tasks and detailed arrangements in the next few years. The exhaustive institutional regulations cover the members' actions and the consortium's work alike. Everybody knows his/her obligations and the penalties for violations of the agreement. Since these provisions were passed at the plenary session and thus are effective to all, the members work together under the formal provisions, leading to a well-operating consortium.

With clear constraints and expectations for the members, the code of conduct constitutes the cornerstone for the operation of SEMATECH. Nonetheless, such exhaustive regulations also have caused some problems. While the consortium is developing and tasks are being carried out, people come to realize that some regulations do not align with reality. SEMATECH has therefore held meetings, along with heated debates, regarding how to modify the code, adding to its operating costs.

(3) Lunch Bunch: Social Network as a Watchdog

Although the book of code of conduct is the cornerstone for the operation of SEMATECH, the social network as a watchdog still plays an auxiliary role, which is demonstrated by an incentive mechanism for the assignees. During the operation of SEMATECH, communication between the consortium and the member companies is realized mainly through the assignees, who will work on behalf of their respective companies to produce a result favorable for them, whenever possible, when the consortium is making a decision on a matter. In the meantime, they are responsible for communicating the consortium's final decision to their respective companies and for urging them to implement it. The assignees' dedicated participation is a precondition for the successful operation of the consortium since they play an important role as bridges for communication.

As we have explained above, however, the assignees tend to be middle and senior managers of their respective companies, where they also hold particular positions. As a result, they are often unavailable for the work of the consortium because of some affairs at their respective companies. Nearly half of the assignees frequently asked for a leave in the early period of the consortium. Their failure to fulfill their obligations had a severe impact on the operation of the consortium. To address this problem, Intel manager Rick Dehmel launched an activity called Lunch Bunch – all the consortium staff members would gather in a meeting room every Wednesday at noon, when they ate sandwiches and participated in a brainstorming session. The topics included a review of the work done in the last week, a preview of the work plan for the next week, the announcement of new things and dissatisfaction among the colleagues. Lunch Bunch would soon turn into a condemnation against the absent assignees, as the attendees would complain against them. It was under this pressure from the peers' opinions that the attendance rate of the assignees greatly increased later on. Lunch Bunch provided an opportunity for regular communication among the consortium staff members, who then became increasingly familiar with one another and formed a social network. An absent member would be rejected and condemned by all the other members of this network, and no assignee dare violate the rules at will because of the pressure from opinions in the network as a powerful watchdog. As the work of the consortium was carried out, the staff members had more opportunities (e.g., meetings and project teams) for face-to-face communication, which further promoted the development of social networking among the members and cooperation among the assignees.

7.5 Comparison between the Chinese and Western Cases

Ostrom proposed a useful theoretical framework for the comparison between the above-stated Chinese and American cases. Her study asserts that, for the self-governance of self-organized units, there are rules at three levels – operational, collective-choice and constitutional-choice rules. At the lowest level are operational rules, which directly affect daily decisions on a multitude of issues, such as: When, where and how to access resources; who is to supervise others' actions and how to do it; what information must be exchanged or must not be released; how to encourage or punish deviant actions and results. In the case of protecting common pool resources, for example, villagers living near a pool may agree, to protect the limited amount of water, that one person can only take one bucket of water from the pool per day and that the taking of any more water is forbidden. To prevent any person from disobeying this rule and taking more water at night, the villagers may go further by designing a monitoring scheme and have a watchdog be on night duty every day. And if someone is really caught stealing water, the villagers may specify a penalty, such as forbidding him from taking water from the pool for three days. Plus, to assure justice and to avoid favoritism, the villagers may design a spot-check system, etc. These detailed and specific regulations all belong to operational rules.

Above operational rules are collective-choice rules, which involve the right to make decisions in the process of developing and changing operational rules. There are examples such as who is to develop operational rules and how to do it and, in the aforementioned case, what the exact allowable daily water consumption is and how to determine it.

At the highest level are constitutional-choice rules, which determine the asset ownership, such as who has the right to decide on matters with respect to the pool, and what kinds of rights a collective may have. In the aforementioned case, the state can specify, if the pool is owned by it, that the pool should be available to all the citizens, making the villagers be not entitled to restrict others from taking water from the pool. Nonetheless, the villagers can decide how to deal with the pool, if it is collectively owned by them. In addition, constitutional-choice rules specify who has the right to decide on collective-choice rules and what kinds of rights the collective may have. As an example, who is entitled to decide on matters related to the common pool, the head of the village or the villagers meeting?

With regard to self-governance rules at the three levels, rules at one level are changed under regulation by the ones at the upper level, according to Ostrom. It is usually more difficult and costly to change rules at a higher level. In this regard, therefore, constitutional-choice rules are the most important ones for self-organized units, whose realization must first be based on matching constitutional-choice rules.

And Ostrom summarized common principles of successful self-governance on the basis of the case analysis. She found out that successful self-organized units always have eight basic characteristics as follows:

(1) Clearly defined boundaries. The boundaries of a common-pool resource (CPR) itself must be specified, and so must individuals or families entitled to take a certain unit of resource from the common pool;

(2) Use and supply rules are consistent with local conditions. It is necessary to define rules regarding the time, location and techniques of use and/or the amount of resource units. These rules should be consistent with local conditions, the needed labor, materials and/or funds as well as the local norms.

(3) Arrangements for collective choice. Most individuals affected by operational rules should be able to participate in modifying these rules;

(4) Supervision. There are people who actively examine the state of the CPR and the user behavior. They are group members responsible for the general users;

(5) Multi-level sanctions. Users who have broken operational rules will probably be sanctioned by other users, officials in charge or both (to an extent depending upon what the breach of rules is about and how severe it is);

(6) A mechanism for conflict settlement. Users and officials in charge can rapidly settle conflicts between them through a low-cost local public forum;

(7) Minimum recognition of the government's power. Users' right for designing their own system is free from challenges posed by the external government authority;

(8) Power-sharing organization. In a multi-level, power-sharing organization, activities such as use, supply, supervision, enforcement, conflict settlement and governance are well-designed.

Ostrom believed that the aforementioned eight principles assure long-term, effective systems for self-organization and self-governance. She noted that these principles designed for governing CPRs can affect incentives and enable users to voluntarily obey operational rules in these systems, to monitor their respective compliance with the rules, and to maintain institutional arrangements for CPRS from generation to generation.

As self-organized units established under different societal backgrounds, the furniture association and SEMATECH also have very different watchdog mechanisms. From the operating perspective, SEMATECH relies more on regulation by formal institutions, while the furniture association follows the idea of "No institutional requirement on any individual or business" – it guides rather than managing the members' behavior by guanxi management. Nonetheless, the social network in SEMATECH also plays a role of supervising the absentees and promoting cooperation; and the furniture association also has basic articles that specify its positioning as well as the basic rights and obligations of the members. We can see, therefore, that the Chinese and western organizations differ from each other in a "more or less" rather than "yes or no" manner.

By analyzing the enabling mechanisms for the operation of the two self-organized units and referring to certain theories, we can find some conclusions as follows:

The phenomenon of critical mass. SEMATECH has a critical mass formed by stakeholders or professional elite on an equal basis. By comparison, such a small group of critical figures, in China, is formed by a capable man as the focal person of a particular social network who mobilizes his/her social relations to join in collective actions. Among them, the capable man assumes functions such as mobilization, structure maintenance and rule design for the self-organization. In the meantime, the qualities of the capable man in terms of role relationships dictate the mode of interactions between the self-organization and external resources. In SEMATECH, there are also influential figures like Noyce and Dehmel who play a critical role; in the furniture association, President Wang is the focal person of the guanxi circle, where he was the one who created the critical mass. Without this focal person, it would be impossible, like when Mr. W was the president, to maintain the furniture association.

Bear the initial costs in return for reputation – a quality that the capable man must have. To maintain his/her reputation, the capable man should not care about rewards or share any benefit, whenever possible, but work to remain reputable. There is no difference in this regard between the two cases.

Devise formal institutions and regulations to establish a self-governance mechanism.

SEMATECH has the four-inch-thick code of conduct and the furniture association has the 1,500-character-long articles of association. There is no difference in this regard between the two organizations, except that the SEMATECH's code of conduct covers almost everything while the articles of the furniture association only propose basic principles and are not that seriously enforced.

Use the social network as a watchdog. The Lunch Bunch in SEMATECH serves as a communication platform for the representatives and staff members, making it an important platform for informal regulations and the reputation mechanism to function. This is the same as in the furniture association, where informal institutions even play a greater watchdog role. To maintain the stable development of the self-organization, the capable man should follow the favor rule, which shows extremely high applicability and practicality in the field of relationships and transactions with familiar ties – where private morals are maintained – despite that certain formal rules are still required. Favor exchanges and informal rules always play a greater role in the operation of the self-organization in the Chinese case and, accordingly, make the regulations of the organization less important.

The distribution mechanism of the organization should assure absolutely fair distribution within it. There is no difference in this principle between SEMATECH and the furniture association, except that the furniture association is unable to realize institutionalization based on consensus. Moreover, with the increase of the membership and public affairs, the favor rule shows a lot of drawbacks during the continuous operation of the self-organization. In this situation, the capable man can meet the expectations of most members only by allowing for the equal sharing of benefits and the universal concept of fairness. The aforementioned conflicts between universalism and particularism always test President Wang's ability to maintain dynamic balance. In other words, the Chinese case has the tendency to govern the self-organization process under rituals, mainly indicated by informal rules and social network, while the western counterpart pay more attention to the governance under "laws", which means the formal institutions and regulations.

Below is a characteristic summary of the phenomenon in Chinese self-organized units:

Start of Self-organization	The phenomenon of capable men (a combination of social and political elite)
Way of Mobilization	Guanxi- and egocentric guanxi network-oriented
Boundaries of Self-organization	Elastic guanxi circles with capable men at the core

Rights & Obligations of critical mass	Bear initial costs – receive a reputation in return – share no extra benefits
Role of capable man in Defining Rules	Definer of formal and tacit rules/ (maybe) destroyer
Source of Mutual Benefit Mechanism	The favor-exchange rule
Resource Distribution	The principle of equal sharing

The above-mentioned is the comparison between only two cases, and it is impossible to find out the general differences in the process of self-organization and in self-governance mechanisms between China and the west by comparing only a few cases, despite that I have collected some other Chinese and western cases for study and have produced very similar comparative results. By comparing these cases, however, we can still make some guesses and propositions that are to be verified by more cases.

In western countries, competition and cooperation among individual and group stakeholders in a relatively diversified and legal environment have gradually led to the "mobilizing elites" and "critical masses" that are led by a small group of power holders and that are good at discussion and cooperation. By comparison, the ongoing societal transformation in China has been in progress with the qualities of "guanxi society", so it will not change the functioning logic of the social structure. Accordingly, a capable man in China generally is the focal person of an established social network and has obvious characteristics of political elite. They are similar to each other in that they possess advantage resources, act as the earliest mobilizers of self-organized units, need to bear the initial costs and receive a reputation in return. Moreover, capable men also need to set values and goals for the self-organized units and participate in defining governance rules. But we have seen in the Chinese case that the capable man build a team around him or her before identifying relationships for mobilization. Moreover, there tend to be insufficient formal rules, while the favor-exchange rule is often the norm followed by the members of the circle. Also, it is necessary to balance favor exchanges and the equal sharing of benefits, as trust will be damaged once they become unbalanced. These principles of guanxi operations will gradually evolve into a series of informal rules governing the self-organized units.

This requires us to think about local qualities in addition to dynamic and historical factors when analyzing the current state of mobilization for self-organization in China. The Chinese behavior is socially oriented (or guanxi-oriented); all the individuals in society are in dense, effective networks; their behavior is more often guided and constrained by informal norms in the group. Since a self-organized unit derives from personal relationships and affections, the favor-exchange rule shows its applicability and practicality. With the increase of the membership and public affairs, however, the favor rule shows a lot of drawbacks during the continuous operation of the self-organization. In this situation, the expectations of most members can only be met by the equal sharing of benefits and the universal concept of fairness. How to balance favor exchange and the equal sharing of benefits has become a challenge for the self-organization.

"The phenomenon of capable men" verifies what Fei Xiaotong referred to as ego-centered guanxi networks in the differential mode of association – a capable man must begin mobilization through his/her guanxi network, build the guanxi circle using existing relationships, and define informal rules. The process of mobilization is often characterized by a capable man mobilizing a group of "small" capable men, who in turn mobilize their respective guanxi networks. In this way, a group gradually expands and shapes up in such a snowballing process. The boundary of the self-organized unit is therefore characterized by elasticity around the capable man's relationships, that is, it shows very obvious signs of a guanxi circle.

In the meantime, factors such as the capable man's social/economic status and code of conduct also dictate the characteristics of the social relationships that he/she mobilizes and of the governance mechanisms of the self-organized unit. And they will go further to affect the capable man's reputation within the social network, before ultimately deciding whether the self-organized unit can achieve the common goal and function for a long period of time or not. Nowadays, the traditional society is changing, but self-organized units in Chinese cities still exhibit the principles of favor exchange and equal sharing that we have observed[①]. As changes occur to urban life and modern economy, however, what are the changes in this process of self-organization that deserve further study and attention?

[①] Sun Yu, Xie Zhaoxia, Fang Zhenping: "On the Effects of the Critical Mass in the Cooperative Mechanism of the Organization", the 8th Conference on the Social Network and Relationship Management, Beijing, July 2012.

Lecture 8 Dynamic Balancing between Governance under Rituals and under Laws

"Do not do to others what you don't want done to yourself." "In the way of the superior man there are four things, to not one of which have I as yet attained[①].-To serve my father, as I would require my son to serve me: to this I have not attained; to serve my prince as I would require my minister to serve me: to this I have not attained; to serve my elder brother as I would require my younger brother to serve me: to this I have not attained; to set the example in behaving to a familiar tie, as I would require him to behave to me: to this I have not attained."

—The Doctrine of Dynamic Balance

Loosened control can bring creativity, elasticity, changeability and initiative in certain situations. For example, the Little John Wayne system in the Hong Kong-based Fung Group, formerly known as the Li & Fung Group, would be extremely effective if it is used to develop new businesses or energize companies. To avoid chaos, however, a hierarchical system must be adopted for the purpose of control. While the Little John Waynes are travelling around like cavalrymen used to do, a huge "wagon train" is required at the corporate headquarters to act as a stabilizer that provides the "cavalry" with logistics, equipment and other support to prevent the Little John Waynes from moving in the wrong direction or even going over to the enemy.

On the one hand, there are constraints from "laws" such as processes, regulations and institutions. Just like the Amoeba Management developed by Kazuo Inamori in KYOCERA Corporation comes with a corresponding set of departmental accounting systems and statements, the Fung Group has built very successful institutions in terms of cash flow, databases and training system. On the other, there are corporate visions, culture and guanxi management to develop real trust in the Fung Group that jointly creates governance under "rituals". In China, Good balance between the two sides enables the do-nothing-against-nature leadership. Without the rule of laws and norms, there will be a series of problems such as closed cliques, infighting and countermeasures against policies from higher levels.

The managerial practice in Chinese organizations is generally ideal for operations based upon power on the one hand and real trust on the other. The abuse of power had better be avoided through laws, whereas real trust should be established through rituals. In other words, good

---

① Confucius admits that these behaviors are even too hard to be achieved for himself.

balance within the organization should be maintained through governance under rituals and laws together. In this context, the "rituals" refer to a set of informal and tacit rules in the organization, as they are needed to establish real trust. In other words, it is necessary to rely on a set of common values and informal norms to establish such relationships. The "laws" refer to a set of formal and written rules.

We always say that we are in a society operating under the rule of human leader. But this is a thorough misunderstanding. This concept of "rule of human leader" exists because "rule of law" is often believed in the west to be contrary to it. This was made very obvious in the Great Essentials upon which the United States is based. Their substance includes four points: The government's power, wherever it is from, can be reclaimed by the people that it rules; a free and independent countries exists to protect the welfare of its people; the government relies on the written constitution, not the power of the human leader; powers must be distributed to the federal, state and local governments and be balanced. Among them, the third point mentions basing the country upon the rule of law as being contrary to basing it upon the rule of human leader. Since Chinese society is not operating under the rule of law, it is believed to be operating under the rule of human leader.

In reality, Chinese society is operating under the rule of rituals, according to Fei Xiaotong.

8.1 Explanations from Local Sociologists

Fei Xiaotong explained, in his book *From the Soil: the Foundations of Chinese Society*, the tradition of the rule of rituals in China using the following story:

A senile father smoked opium, to which his eldest son, let's say, Tom, objected. Nonetheless, his second eldest son, let's say, Jack, who was an idle man, also smoked opium and encouraged his father to do so in order to gain a share. Since he was not allowed to criticize his father, Tom beat Jack very severely. Jack passed the buck to father, so an enraged Tom even cursed the latter. This dispute was later on submitted to the village council for mediation by the squire. Since mediation had nothing to do, in this context, with settlement in the legal sense, Jack was not demanding compensation for being beaten, and Tom also was not asking for living separately from his father and Jack because of financial burden. Instead, they submitted the dispute only to see who was right and who was wrong. It turned out that the squire said, as usual, that this was a scandal for the whole village, before preaching interpersonal ethics. At last, he decided that Jack was the black sheep of the family and should be expelled from the village; Tom failed to observe filial piety and should be punished by inviting the other villagers to dinner as a gesture of apology for his fault. And their father was criticized once again for having failed to properly educate his sons and for smoking opium. The father and sons thus accepted the penalties and returned home. Since he was a scholar, Fei Xiaotong was believed to be learned and reasonable and therefore was also invited to help determine who was right or wrong, despite that he was an outsider who had come to the village for research. After the end of the mediation, the squire complained to Fei, saying that "People are morally deteriorating day by day and are no longer what they used to be."

The rule of law stresses that "man governs the country by law", where law is developed from constitution. In other words, interactions between human beings are regulated by legal provisions. Given the tradition of staying away from lawsuits, however, Chinese people seldom wanted to file lawsuits with the local county governors and, instead, would ask the local patriarchs, or persons known for wisdom and virtues, for deciding who was right or wrong. Laws stress rights protection, but the above-mentioned story was neither about Tom demanding property damages because he had spent much money nor about the father claiming compensation for a damaged reputation. In contrast, the squire emphasized, when judging who was right or wrong, that the local morals were deteriorating. That was why he began mediation by preaching ethics and ended it by "punishing" the senile father through verbal education to reform him and by "punishing" Tom by having him acknowledge his fault and apologize for it.

The rule of rituals is therefore about regulating interpersonal relationships and interactions through ethics and customs. Fei Xiaotong thought that the concept of "rule of human leader" was dubious because it sounded like interpersonal relationships and interactions could simply be regulated by an order said by the leader. In reality, there were few Chinese leaders who were able to govern the whole country simply through their charisma; most of them were also not tyrants who governed the country with dictatorial power, but instead were more often patriarchs who emphasized educational power. In a society under the rule of rituals, the legitimacy of a regime comes more often from educational power than from dictatorial or consensual power. This is because rituals as informal, unwritten rules rely more heavily on human beings' self-consciousness and self-discipline so as to maintain order. Impart these norms to them then becomes the top priority. The greatest significance of patriarchism lies in education – a set of norms are imparted into human beings to create a good public-opinion environment.

8.2 Laws vs. Rituals

8.2.1 The Rule by Law in China: Focus on Simplicity

Chinese leaders generally are skillful at playing roles of the patriarch and the matriarch: One leader in the organization often plays the role of a strict patriarch who enforces all the corporate regulations and orders; some other leader plays the role of a gentle matriarch who influences the employees through education. The head of a company typically plays the role of the matriarch to make the company full of affection and care, while the second highest-ranking official plays the role of the law enforcement official who carries out supervision to see if there is any non-compliance, and, when necessary, punishes the "wrongdoer." After the employee is cornered by the "tyrannical" second highest-ranking official, the head will come to comfort him/her so that he/she will become thankful and more willing to work. But such an arrangement also comes with risks, as the head may become ceremonial if he/she is always kind to the employees and the second highest-ranking official always takes punitive measures to them: The employees all know that the former is a nice guy while the latter is the one who actually dictates their career development in the company. Gradually, the second highest-ranking official will become the de-facto power holder in the organization. We may say, therefore, that the best method is to have "laws" play the role of the "bad guy" and to specify all the penalties beforehand.

Wise Chinese leaders indeed are fully aware of how important it is to properly use laws, and everyone, including him/herself, needs to obey the laws. To assure that laws are obeyed throughout the organization, it is necessary to first realize consistency – the head must take the lead in obeying them so as to make them respectable. And why is it advisable to be good at using laws? This is because all the people will submit willingly to the leader's management if he or she rewards or punishes them by law in an impartial and consistent manner. In reality, the rule of law did exist in Chinese history, only that the laws were not made on the basis of a democratic agreement. At times when the government was well governed, the emperor was not able to do whatever he wanted to. Instead, his administrative orders needed to be reviewed and discussed by the high-rank officers for their consent. In the reign of Emperor Taizong（AD 626-649）of the Tang Dynasty, Wei Zheng, a high-ranking government official known for daring to expressing opinions even if they might make the emperor unhappy, could even openly reject Emperor Taizong's orders for the purpose of review, since he has the right to do so according the laws of Tang Dynasty. That is why we said at the beginning of this paragraph that good Chinese leaders indeed are fully aware of how important it is to obey and properly use laws.

With regard to organizational system design in China, however, the focus is always on the simplicity of laws. Specifically, laws are implementable only if they are simple and clear and if the leaders set themselves good examples for obeying laws. Unfortunately, there is now a trend in China that there are a growing number of laws with increasing complexity. Laws, if cumbersome, generally cannot be implemented and end up working only in two aspects in China– for the government to clarify its position and for some politicians to find fault with other people. An excess of legal provisions, many of which are overly stringent or stiff, will end up turning almost everyone into a criminal. The ruler would take advantage of "unsolved problems" of particular officials to constrain them. This would result in a scenario where righteous persons were constrained in every aspect while petty ones, or those who were good at getting close to and relying on dignitaries, became dominant. Fei Xiaotong also said that petty persons would become dominant once Chinese society is ruled under overly stringent laws.

There used to be a "Last Day" phenomenon in China – the laws would become increasingly stringent as a regime was approaching its end, whereas they were very loose when the regime was in the prime of its life, but could be well implemented once they were made. For example, during the reigns of Emperors Wen (BC 180-157) and Jing (BC 157-141) of the Western Han Dynasty (BC 202-AD 8), a period of peace and prosperity, all the people, even including princes, would receive the same punishment for the same crime, which in turn led to clean politics and good order throughout the country. In contrast, at the end of Western Han Dynasty, everybody would be willing to become petty persons once they were prone to receive punishment as a result of cumbersome, rigorous laws. This was because only petty persons could lead a good life in this situation thanks to their ability to secure personal gains in a dishonest manner.

During the late Eastern Han Dynasty (AD 25-220), Liu Xiao, the general commander of the garrison of the capital appointed by politician and warlord Dong Zhuo, was angered by decadence and dissatisfactory education in society and, hence, conducted investigations on failure to observe filial piety, disloyalty to one's superior and lack of respect for one's elder brother among both officials and ordinary people. Anyone who had committed any of such wrongdoing would be beheaded and his/her property confiscated. It turned out that this cruelty caused great panic and a great many people took advantage of it by producing false evidence against each other. Consequently, the city of Chang'an, the then capital of China and now known as the city of Xi'an, became a world of horror full of wrongful convictions. When meeting on the street, even people who knew well about each other would do no more than taking a look at one another, without daring to say a word. Rituals in Chinese society were rooted in four essentials – filial piety, respect for one's elder brother, loyalty to one's monarch, and faith to one's familiar ties, but it was impossible to promote the four essentials through law enforcement. If persons who were disloyal to their monarch or failed to observe filial piety must be punished by law, then this law would become a bad law that was not only impossible to be implemented but would also cause the people to produce false evidence against each other. Consequently, the people would doubt each other and, hence, make trust disappear from society.

A good law is in itself very simple, but it should be perfectly obeyed at all levels, plus flexibility beyond the legal provisions. In the Qing Dynasty (AD 1644-1911), inscribed on the tablet hanging in the county governor's office was not the typical "Ming Jing Gao Xuan" (literally, "Loftily hangs the bright mirror", which means that the official is honest and perspicacious in judging a case), but "Tian Li Ren Qing Guo Fa" (literally, "The principles of nature, human affection, national laws"). Since both the principles of nature laws and social norms are placed before national laws, we can see that certain room beyond laws should be left for both of them. And this room should be defined by rituals.

8.2.2 Order under the Rule of Ritual

Now that there are a self-organized group of people, both affection and trust are indispensable, and the group must be governed under rituals: Remembering others' favors, seeking chances to return favors, being willing to take risks or even sacrifice some private benefits for one's familiar ties, being fair and righteous, and showing benevolence. There must be a set of group norms to define what can, or cannot, be done. And this set of norms is developed on the basis of rituals.

The process of building a self-organized unit, as we have discussed above, can be summarized into the following stages: Build a social network; create a small circle; the members begin to identify with their small circle; establish a group goal and begin to take collective actions; lastly and most importantly, group norms – that is, order under the rule of rituals in the self-organized unit – come into being for the purpose of self-management while collective actions are in progress. Furthermore, a collective watchdog mechanism will then appear within the small group to punish individuals who have violated the group norms.

Briefly, the self-organization process mush lead to a self-governance mechanism. The self-governance mechanism researched by Ostrom tends to be a set of rules, including constitutional-choice, collective-choice and operational rules (Ostrom, 1990; 1998), whereas in China, it tends to be a set of unwritten, informal norms.

Governance under rituals, or governance realized through self-organization, has a very unique set of internal behavioral logic. Governance within Chinese self-organized units is generally based on unwritten rules. The members of a self-organized unit can supervise each other since they can get to know each other in a small guanxi circle; somebody, once he/she violates a certain rule, will receive immediate condemnation and moral stress from the other members, and will even take the risk of being expelled from the group. These punitive measures are able to effectively constrain the members' behavior. In addition, such supervision is made at a very low cost, since it is jointly carried out by all the other members of the group; and it is very effective since the members of the small group know well about each other, making information asymmetry impossible. Accordingly, governance under rituals can establish order within the self-organization at a low cost.

In villages of traditional Chinese society, there were no institutions specializing in maintaining public order, such as the police and written regulation, but most villages were able to maintain long-term peace. One of the main reasons was that governance under rituals was an ancient practice in traditional villages. Every villager other than the village's patriarch played the role, even without their knowledge, of a traditional order maintainer who carried out supervision all the time and reported non-compliance, if any. Accordingly, a strong supervisory force could be created with no need for law enforcement officials.

Even in modern society, effective moral supervision generally is realized by community members. With regard to communities ranging from professional or industrial ones, such as those of doctors, scholars or other specialists, to rural communities, urban apartment complexes, interest groups or online groups, it is up to the people in these communities to decide whether the acts of other members of their communities have violated the community norms, or departed from the basic professional ethics, or not. Unfortunately, however, a current problem in China happens to be with intra-circle supervision – government officials cover up for each other; tacit rules prevail in circles, for example. For example, the media, known as "the masses' voice" or "an uncrowned king", should play the important role of disclosing the truth and acting as a watchdog, is short of effective internal ethics and supervision. Fake-journalists and fake-news appear frequently. This has caused an overall lack of trust across society. We are now in a truth-hungry society where Internet users who are inclined to make groundless guesses may spread various rumors and guesses at will, whereas the voice of circle members who know the truth is unheard. In other words, today's China has yet transformed itself from the traditional modes of governance under rituals into the modern ones.

Both the establishment of informal norms and supervision rely on the general awareness of morality. Only on this basis can a self-organized unit develop its "rituals" in accordance with the members' moral consensus, relevant customs and community specificity. What can be supervised by public opinions is the "rituals" within the circle. We are in urgent need of calling for morality in order to create a good overall social environment. And we are in even more urgent need of building our society's capacity of self-organization so as to supervise and uphold morality with opinions within the small group, because a group of people who know well about each other is free from information asymmetry. Only in this way can the watchdog and reputation mechanisms become effective. Attempts to uphold morality by public opinion generally yield nothing but rumors and vilifications because of insufficient information, hypes by the media, and distorting reporting.

8.3 Governance under Rituals and Laws Together: Local Cases in China

Good Chinese management is characterized by governance under rituals and laws together. Business managers often find out that the power granted by the formal institutions must be used since it is impossible to keep people under control with only kindness and without authority; but that it cannot be overly used, or they will not receive the loyalty of and support from their subordinates. How then can they use it properly?

Next, I would like to explain how governance under rituals and laws together is realized in Chinese enterprises with the result of my research on how high-tech vendors govern outsourcing transactions. This case again is not within an organization; rather, it is related to the subcontracting network outside an organization. The process of governing outsourcing transactions can be divided into six workflows as follows:

(1) Identify the vendors;

(2) Sign purchase contracts;

(3) Bargain (to set prices);

(4) Inspect and receive products;

(5) Manage the supplied goods and production (for example, such activities include manufacturing products for a particular order faster than usual or prioritizing it over others);

(6) Make an assessment.

For the part of producers that use outsourcing services, there are two biggest uncertainties. Firstly, supply quality is inconsistent. The overall product quality will ultimately be affected if the quality of key parts supplied by the outsourcing service providers is problematic. Secondly, the supply is not stable. Production in high-tech manufacturing tends to be managed in real time. In other words, the high-tech vendor has few or even no products in stock and conducts production under the principle of "Supply as needed." Components supplied by the outsourcing service providers will be sent to the plants for production as soon as they arrive. Accordingly, the production will be suspended if the supply is unstable and delayed. This means great losses to vendors that operate assembly lines of final products.

In these workflows, high-tech vendors will make full use of "power" and "favors" as two instruments, in addition to increasing efficiencies and reducing risks through formal mechanisms (including standard business processes, written regulations, supply chain management software, etc.), to realize governance under rituals and laws together. First of all, why is there a phenomenon of governance under laws, the written regulations in this case? There is indeed a power imbalance between final-product producers and outsourcing service providers. For smaller providers that rely on its orders to survive, the producer generally will require them to satisfy its internal standards and rules; and for powerful ones that make critical components (such as chipmaker Intel), the producer will have to follow their rules. The gaps in power allow the producer to force particular outsourcing service providers to obey its "laws." On the other hand, however, the producer cannot always rely on its formal mechanisms to force the providers to do what is told.

With regard to high-tech manufacturing, inherent characteristics of this industry result in foreign companies' being less competitive than their Chinese counterparts. High-tech manufacturing features very short and violent business cycles and very rapid technology changes; that indicates the high uncertainty of environment. Excessive parts bought in the last cycle, if any, may become useless in the next one, because products are updated or upgraded very rapidly, with ever-changing designs and appearance. And there also are great changes in the demand for products, as they are prone to be oversupplied at this time and undersupplied at another. It is in this situation that rapid change and quick response becomes crucial. Good buyers in the final-product producers must meet two requirements. Firstly, they can assure component supply even in season, so that the assembly line will not be suspended. Secondly, they can get lower prices out of season. Among which, the first requirement is even more important. Accordingly, good buyers will intentionally leave room for favors while they are trying to get lower prices out of season, thereby assuring that their companies can make products for particular orders faster than usual or prioritize these orders over others in season.

Take Workflows 3 and 5 for example. On the one hand, there are a series of standard business processes for placing orders and managing supplies, according to ISO 9000 and the producer's regulations. On the other hand, there should be some room for flexible operations in these processes. The prices of high-tech products typically begin to go down shortly after they are placed in the markets, together with changes in the prices of components, which occur once every two or three months according to the usual industry practice. In this process, buyers generally will favor the outsourcing service providers intentionally. As an example, postponements can be made: The buyers begin negotiations for lower prices at the beginning of a certain month and will not cut them until two months later, thereby allowing the outsourcing service providers to make higher profits for two more months. In this situation, the buyers will deliberately complain to the providers and let them remember the favors in mind. And later one, when it is in season, the providers may have their employees work at night to fulfill the buyers' demand (so that the latter ones' companies are able to make products for particular orders faster than usual) even when the factories are already operating with full workload. Alternatively, the providers will first supply goods to the producers to whom they have favor debts – they will prioritize the latter ones' orders over others. In contrast, buyers who left no room for favors during price negotiations out of season may receive revenge from the outsourcing service providers in season – their orders will not be prioritized and, thus, their companies may have to suspend production. Buyers who cannot assure timely supply will then be regarded as being incompetent and, hence, be fired. Since they need to make products for particular orders faster than usual or prioritize these orders over others in season, producers should leave sufficient room, at usual times, for guanxi management, and deal with the outsourcing service providers under "rituals". The providers call vendors that abuse power and that leave little or even no room for favors "robbers"; they generally will postpone supplying goods to force such vendors to suspend production.

Governance under rituals and laws together is also reflected in Workflow 4, inspecting the goods. There are usually a standard process for inspecting the supplies and an industry-accepted allowable error probability in the process of goods inspection. A batch of goods will be regarded as non-compliant if it exceeds this probability. Producers tend to take a moderate approach when governing the outsourcing service providers. If the error probability is found to be unacceptably high, the producers will allow the providers to take the goods back and   re-inspect them with their internal standards to avoid errors caused by differences from the instruments used by the two sides. The producers will return the goods only when they are found once again to be non-compliant. And they will not necessarily decide immediately to replace the providers, with which they have cooperated for a long period of time and established good relationships, even after they have returned the goods to the latter ones once and again. Instead, both sides may have their engineers discuss to jointly solve the problems. And the final-product producers may even send people to the component providers to help them satisfy relevant standards. So, in high-tech manufacturing, there are certain industry standards, on the one hand, and favors and benevolence, on the other. Such a practice assures strong cooperative and trust-based relationships between producers and outsourcing service providers, thereby enabling flexibility and speed.

8.4 Paternalistic Leadership with Benevolence, Authoritarianism and Morality Together

Now that Chinese management is characterized by governance under rituals and laws together, good Chinese leaders must be paternalistic ones with benevolence, authoritarianism and morality together. This is what Farh and Cheng (2000) called "paternalistic leadership". Being kind and authoritative alike indeed is commonly known as the art of playing patriarch and matriarch at the same time. A good leader knows that playing patriarch is as needed as is playing matriarch in the organization. In other words, he/she knows how to balance power and trust. On the one side, the "authoritarianism" of a good leader is based on stringent law enforcement. The leader should know when to adhere to the principle of "business is business" to suggest that there is no favor beyond laws. Such strict accordance with rules will naturally establish his/her authority within the organization; and the employees will submit willingly to his/her management since he/she deals with them in a fair and consistent manner. Unfortunately, a great many leaders have a misunderstanding of "authoritarianism", as they think it means nothing but being bossy and abusing power. In reality, abusing power will not establish the leader's authority, but will make the employees seemingly compliant but actually resistant to his/her management.

On the other side, a good leader knows the importance of governance under rituals. He/she should keep some room for favor-exchanges and, at usual times, pay more attention to being kind to others. By doing favors at usual times, the leader can make the employees grateful   and more willing to help to realize his/her dream. In fact, the art of leadership by being kind and authoritative alike is common also in the west, only that the "benevolence" of Chinese leaders is characterized, to a higher extent, by favor exchanges.

Nonetheless, "morality leadership" is most characteristic of China. The morality leadership in this context, as we have discussed above, of course, does not require the leader to make himself/herself a sage and to advocate high moral standards. Instead, it first means that the leader himself/herself should follow the rules and the culture of the organization, that is, its rituals, or its unwritten, informal norms. In other words, the leader should set him/her a perfect example in obeying the rules and the culture that he/she wants to establish in the organization. This is somewhat like the so-called values-based leadership in management theories.

Fei Xiaotong said that the educational power was an important power that leaders held in Chinese society, where patriarchy was one of the traditions. When a patriarch was judging a case, the most important thing for him was not to determine the ownership of benefits through his wisdom, but to rely on his prestige to set a perfect model example for the people. A leader who holds the education power is similar in status with the queen of the United Kingdom, who need not do too much but only stay high as the sources of perfect morality examples and the educational power.

A leader has many things to do, however, before realizing such do-nothing leadership. First of all, the leader should polish his/her own character and constrain himself/herself so that he/she is able to stand for the culture, norms, vision and values of the organization. By set him/her a perfect example, the leader generally is able to make the employees more confident in the organization and to better inspire them to work hard. That is why the Doctrine of Dynamic Balance takes cultivating oneself as the beginning of Chinese management.

8.4.1 The Implications from the Chinese History

Hong Kong scholar Larry Jiing-Lih Farh and Taiwanese scholar Po-Hsun Cheng accurately grouped leaders into eight types through benevolence, authoritarianism and morality as three dimensions. The eight types include: "Wise leaders" with high authoritarianism, high benevolence and high morality; "heads of gangs" with high authoritarianism, high benevolence and low morality; "honest officials" with high authoritarianism, low benevolence and high morality; "tyrants" with high authoritarianism, low benevolence and low morality; "kind leaders" with low authoritarianism, high benevolence and high morality; "moral paradigms" with low authoritarianism, low benevolence and high morality; pamperers with low authoritarianism, high benevolence and low morality; "mediocre leaders" with low authoritarianism, low benevolence and low morality.

Among the eight types, "kind leaders" are the most ideal type of leaders in the eyes of Chinese people, according to the findings of a survey – nearly half of its samples selected this option. "Wise leaders" only took the second place, as they were popular with about one fourth of the samples. "Moral paradigms" took the third place. "Honest officials" only took the fourth place, and the persons who selected this option were greatly outnumbered by those who selected any of the first three options. The percentages of those who selected any of the remaining four options were all insignificant. Interestingly, pamperers with low authoritarianism, high benevolence and low morality were not popular, which suggests how wise the Chinese are. Leaders of this type will think of how the people around them feel, but it is very difficult for them to make right decisions. Consequently, they will end up benefiting a small group of people around them at the sacrifice of the vast majority.

Emperor Dezong （AD 779-805） of the Tang Dynasty was such a typical example. The Tang Dynasty was already on the decline after the rebellion of An Lushan and Shi Siming (AD 755-783; the latter was a general of the Tang Dynasty who followed the former in rebelling against Tang Dynasty), but the government still decided to greatly expand royal gardens. It expropriated massive farmland without compensating the farmers who had thus lost their land. Emperor Dezong was greatly moved when a rural farmer cried and complained to him during his visit to a certain place. He then immediately exempted this farmer's family from taxes. It seemed kind but indeed was unwise of him to do so. On one hand, he did not rethink the wrong decision of expanding royal gardens, nor did he act to investigate whether certain officials had taken advantage of this opportunity for corruption, or had failed to fulfill their duties by protecting the farmers from any resulting losses. On the other hand, he damaged the stringency of rule of law by exempting only this family from taxes without considering more farmers who had lost land. With regard to leaders in the pamperers' type, a common phenomenon is that "the crying children receive milk." Such a leader has a group of devoted followers around him/her, and they will become arrogant toward all the other people since they were favored by the leader. In contrast, officials and employees who are less close to the leader can do nothing but complain. It is impossible for such a person to properly manage any organization.

We can see from the above-mentioned preferences that high morality is always a quality indispensable for a good Chinese leader who is able to realize long-term prosperity and peace. Since values, vision and culture are at the core of governance under rituals, leaders who practice what they preach and who truly believe in the vision are the only ones who can communicate the vision; and leaders who set themselves perfect examples for the other people are the only ones who can establish good norms for organizations. And morality leadership seems all the more critical for managing an organization or a government. Accordingly, Chinese leaders must first be sincere in their thoughts and polish their own character.

8.4.2 Balancing between Benevolence and Law Enforcement

Being benevolent and authoritative alike is a quality of leaders good at developing new businesses. Being authoritative is about relying on laws to create rewarding/punishment criteria; being benevolent is about favors, but it sometimes comes into conflict with governance under laws. This also is the dilemma between favors and equal sharing in Zhai Xuewei's theory.

Dang Renhong was one of the key persons who helped Li Yuan, Emperor Taizong's father, found the Tang Dynasty, before following Emperor Taizong of the Tang Dynasty. With exceptional ability and performance at work, Dang Renhong was regarded highly by Li Shimin, the real name of Emperor Taizong. Unfortunately, he was very greedy and found to defalcate a lot of money. Dang was to be beheaded according to the laws of the Tang Dynasty, but Li Shimin spoke for him before all the ministers（AD 624）, emphasizing that the national laws were set by the Providence and thus must not be damaged because of private benevolence, but that he didn't have the heart to see a senile Dang who had spent all his life working for public good be beheaded. Therefore, Li Shimin asked whether it was possible to make an exception for Dang. To persuade the ministers, Li Shimin swore that he would sleep on a straw mat and fast for three days for a punishment on himself. Later on, Fang Xualing, one of the most celebrated chancellors of the Tang Dynasty, said that the emperor always had the power to grant amnesty and, hence, that Li Shimin really didn't have to torment himself like this. It was not until then did Li Shimin issued a decree to condemn himself, acknowledging that he had failed to see through this man and that he had damaged the national laws for private ties. Besides apologizing to the people across the country, Li Shimin reduced Dang Renhong to a commoner and expelled him to Qinzhou, a place far away from the Capital.

Another good example is Zhuge Liang (AD 181-234; he was a chancellor of the state of Shu Han during the Three Kingdoms period. He is popularly recognized as the greatest and most accomplished strategist of his era) ordering to behead Ma Su (he was a military general and strategist of the state of Shu Han). Ma Su was the chief advisor to Zhuge Liang and devised tactics that became well-known afterward, such as "It is better to win the heart of the people than to capture the city" and "Catch and release Meng Huo seven times to win his heart." Nonetheless, Liu Bei, the first Emperor of Shu Han (AD 221-263), cautioned Zhuge Liang, before he died, that "Ma Su is not as capable as he appears, so never let him do anything important." In other words, Ma Su was no more than an advisor and was unable to carry out specific tasks, so he should never act as a leader.

Unfortunately, Zhuge Liang misused Ma Su's talent by letting the latter, who was good at devising tactics, go to command the vanguard in Jieting （a place in the frontier; AD 228）. It turned out that after arriving at Jieting, Ma Su underperformed expectations, as he focused on trivialities and was demanding to his subordinates, making the soldiers unwilling to execute his orders. Furthermore, this wise guy acted against an order of Zhuge Liang by giving up the water source and the castle and camping at the top of the mountain. At last, he lost Jieting to the enemy, who had the water source cut off and forced the Shu Han army, which had just come out of the borderline, to retreat.

The above-mentioned tragedy in which a weeping Zhuge Liang ordered to behead Ma Su has become a well-known drama in China. More importantly, however, Zhuge Liang swore to regard Ma Su's mother as his own and to support her for the rest of her life. To assure that orders would always be executed and military laws obeyed, Zhuge Liang had Ma Su beheaded, but, as he felt that he owed the latter a favor, he vowed to support Ma's mother, thereby showing his benevolence with Ma Su and making the latter no longer feel worried.

In the story preceding the one about Zhuge Liang, Li Shimin found from the laws the power to grant amnesty (extra options were possible only if the laws were focused on simplicity and flexibility), but damaged the justice of the national laws for private ties. He therefore apologized to the people by issuing a decree to condemn him and by punishing himself through fasting. By so doing, Li Shimin managed to balance laws and private benevolence. And we also can see from the story about Zhuge Liang that he gave top priority to the military laws, but that he also allowed for the private ties. The only difference was that he maintained justice before doing something personal to allow for the private ties.

Why did Li Shimin put private ties before the national laws, while Zhuge Liang prioritizes the military laws over the private ties? This was related to the overall environments they were in, rather than their respective character or relationships with the other person. Li Shimin began to advocate the rule of rituals since he was already living in a peaceful world and wanted to maintain long-term peace. He therefore did this to exemplify the behavior characterized by gratitude and respect or morality. By contrast, Zhuge Liang was living in the late Eastern Han Dynasty known for a lack of discipline, so establishing discipline was the most important thing at that time. This was why Zhuge Liang gave top priority to the military laws.

Governance under rituals and laws together, and balancing between benevolence and law enforcement, are always major issues in Chinese management that challenge managers' wisdom.

Lecture 9 Conclusion: The Significance of Chinese Managerial Philosophies

To sum up the preceding lectures, Chinese managerial philosophies under the doctrine of dynamic balance, first of all, value self-discipline and guanxi management, which in turn aims to establish trust within a group of people. A person needs to dynamically balance the expressive and instrumental motives in his/her relationships with others, to seek balance between particularistic favor exchanges and the universalistic principle of equal sharing, and to maintain balance between the use of power and trust building. This will enable the person to realize a great many instrumental objectives, long-term and short-term, while strengthening real trust in a continuous manner.

A person operates these relationships so as to: Join the leader's circle where he/she can rely on the collective power to secure resources, plus more opportunities for favor exchanges; and form an egocentric guanxi circle, which is the cornerstone for realizing personal, long-term objectives. But good circle operations also require dynamic balance between the opening and closing of the circle's boundaries, as well as between special favors within the circle and fair distribution outside it. Only with good dynamic balance is it possible to maintain a resizable circle, close intra-circle cooperation and the harmony inside and outside the guanxi circle. And only in this way can a person mobilize, or not mobilize, his/her egocentric guanxi network resources, more or less, in a very flexible manner. This is why the Chinese are flexible, changeable and adaptive to environmental changes.

A person operates the circle so as to be enfeoffed – that is, being allowed to self-organize a fully or half independent team, subunit or organization. An organizational or government leader also should know the philosophy of "loosened control" – only when people are given opportunities for self-organization, can various things coexist in the system and can the system itself stay elastic, changeable, adaptive and permanent. A system is an organization from the perspective of organizational leader, while it is referred to a society from the view of a governmental leader.

But how can we loosen control without causing chaos? It is also necessary to maintain dynamic balance between loosened and tightened control. We should think about the specific situation before deciding whether to adopt the principle of self-organization-based governance more often than the hierarchy-based governance mechanism, or the other way round. In the meantime, we should check to see whether the combination of different governance mechanisms is out of balance. The system will be damaged by overemphasis, or under-emphasis, on any single aspect.

To loosen control without causing chaos, it is also necessary to dynamically balance the "rituals" as informal norms and the "laws" as formal rules. In other words, we should carry out governance under laws and rituals that work together in a complementary manner. The laws set the minimally acceptable behavior and uphold the equity rule; loosened control will bring higher freedom; the rituals prevent the self-organization from the abuse of freedom. This is what is meant by the benevolence, authoritarianism and morality leadership stressed by traditional Chinese wisdom.

How then do the aforementioned Chinese managerial philosophies differ from their western counterparts? This is a question that is big and difficult to answer, so I can hardly provide a comprehensive answer. But I'll give it a try.

I think the primary difference is neither a matter of true or false, nor a matter of yes or no. All the organizational phenomena in China have been covered by western theories, and we have practiced most of those. The difference lies in what the extent is and where to start.

Differences between Chinese and western management are neither the ones between collectivism and individualism, nor the ones between scientific and human-oriented management. Collectivism also exists in the West, only that identity is built more upon factors such as race, class, gender, occupation and age. Relatively speaking, of course, the West places more emphasis on individualism. Collectivism in China more often manifests itself as the behavior in guanxi circles. The phenomena of the rule of rituals also occur in the West, where people also value cultures and visions and devise institutions to promote self-organization, such as the internal startup system and self-directed teams that have emerged more recently.

Nonetheless, people in the West place more emphasis on processes, regulations and institutions, and focus their managerial thinking on planning and control. Since the hypothesis of economic man is preset in such managerial philosophies, organizations can be rationally designed and controlled – this is the thinking from the rational system perspective (Scott and Davis. 2007). This is why modern management thoughts, which started from Max Weber's theory of hierarchy and Frederick Taylor's scientific management movement, are thinking that put emphasis on what W. Richard Scott (Scott and Davis. 2007) referred to as the "rational system". But this set of thoughts is continually corrected by the natural system. Examples include *The Functions of the Executive* by Chester Barnard (Barnard, 1938), Hawthorne experiments and the human relations movement by Elton Mayo (Mayo, 1945), institutionalism of Philip Selznick (Selznick, 1943) and even Granovetter's social network theory.

Chinese management happens to be opposite to its western counterpart. It circles around the natural system since we always look at the principles of management from the perspective of Daoism – "The Way models itself on nature." Accordingly, the natural system respects the sociality and non-rationality of human beings, and emphasizes naturally formed social structures. As a result, network structure and self-organization are employed as the main governance structures; problems are addressed through spontaneous cooperation among members. The Chinese are therefore, naturally, more familiar with network forms of   organizations.

It is impossible, of course, to realize good management by relying on any single governance model, whether in the West or in China. Instead, merits of one system relative to the other are considered. Good management is often characterized by a combination of the rational and natural systems and by the use of the three governance structures – hierarchy, network and market – in a complementary manner.

Western management centers on the rational system, along with support from the natural system. Accordingly, western organizations usually place more emphasis on businesses than on people, and, thus, pay more attention to business planning, implementation, assessment and rewarding/punishment in accordance with their respective processes, rules and institutions. By setting organizational structures, rules/institutions and processes, managers turned employees into "screws" in the processes. Later on, however, the managers found out that these "screws" had begun to show dissatisfaction by working slowly and disobeying their orders. It was not until then that a series of elements of human-oriented management, such as employee care and vision management, were developed to increase the job satisfaction as well as senses of belonging and achievement of the "screws", before finally encouraging them to work.

Corresponding to the rational system is the natural system, which believes in the assumptions about human nature of social persons. Specifically, it believes that people need relationships, small groups as well as the senses of belonging and trust, so their association occurs naturally; and that great organizational phenomena can never be rationally designed or controlled. Chinese management, which is social-oriented since its outset, centers more on the natural system, along with support from the rational system. Accordingly, the Chinese tend to manage people before managing businesses, as they emphasize that "If there is no problem with people, then there is no problem with businesses." Chinese management pays more attention to judging a person, getting him mentally ready for work, building trust relations, and assigning him a suitable job, before empowering him in the hope that "I achieve success without having to do anything." Chinese leaders will not specify the details of every job, but carry out guanxi management in the early stage – the job is up to you after trust is established. This is why the best leader is the leader who does nothing against nature. In the case of Chinese management, self-organization is first recognized, because efficiencies are from self-organization and rituals rather than from bureaucracy, regulations, institutions, plans and controls.

This is the difference of "more or less", rather than "yes or no", between Chinese and western management thoughts. Chinese managerial wisdom puts more emphasis on self-discipline, guanxi management, circle operations and self-organization-based governance than bureaucratic principles.

But we also can't help asking: Why is China supposed to have a centralized government since the ancient times? And why did it have world's largest hierarchical organization till the 19th century? The rational system, when in Chinese organizations, aims to better regulate the minimally acceptable behavior while increasing cooperativeness and real trust in the process of managing people. In other words, the laws are intended to support rituals. And we all know that although these self-organized units are of course very vigorous, the vigor will probably cause chaos in the end. The chaos in turn will bring about infighting and even fragmentation, or worse, a dogfight. To avoid this scenario and maintain stability among self-organized units, we must have a hierarchical organization to regulate minimally acceptable behaviors. In this process of hierarchical control, however, China still places much emphasis on the order under the rule of rituals as well as guidance through its values and culture; and it gives top priority to guanxi management.

Although it emphasizes self-organization, Chinese management still needs to maintain the balance between the hierarchical power and self-organization. How to get it done? The clerisy, for example, played a role of bridges between the lower and upper levels in the practices of Chinese political organizations. The essence of Chinese management lies in emphasizing the balance between "the emperor's power" and "the gentry's power," where the former represents the top-down hierarchical control, and the latter, the bottom-up self-organization.

This traditional managerial thought can be traced back to the Chinese political organizations, which were characterized by the emperor's power having little influence in the countryside, as there were no control mechanisms that represented the central power in places below the level of counties. Instead, all the villages, which generally represent about 90% Chinese in the ancient time, were fundamentally autonomous. Local squires played a crucial role in this aspect. Fei Xiaotong noted in his book *Imperial Power and Gentry's Power* that in the traditional social structure of China, the gentry played a special role. On the one hand, they might be retired officials who had more or fewer ties with organizations that represented the emperor's power, so they were able to influence decisions made by upper levels. On the other hand, they were the leaders of local self-organized units and thus were responsible for maintaining local interests. The emperor's power often conflicted with local interests in particular matters since it was always inclined to expand itself and extract local resources. And the local gentry happened to be in the interface between the top-down hierarchical power and the bottom-up power of self-organization, making them a shield that protected local interests from being damaged by the emperor's power. The gentry's egocentric guanxi networks played the key role in balancing these two types of power.

With regard to the traditional political landscape in China, Confucians went for the separation of the Confucian orthodoxy and centralized governance. Intellectuals represented the Confucian orthodoxy; and the emperor, centralized governance. The Chinese pay much more attention to officials than to petty civil servants since the ancient times. Keju, or Chinese national civil service examinations, was largely about classics and poetry, which suggests that they focused on personal morals rather than capabilities. Capable men could be appointed as petty civil servants, who were technical officials and received little attention in traditional China. The Confucian orthodoxy was represented by officials, or a group of intellectual officials, who were supposed to set moral values for the people and the right direction for their lives. Shouldered with the responsibility for constraining the emperor's power, they tried to use theories of the Confucian orthodoxy as weapons in order to maintain the balanced governance. The Confucian orthodoxy advocated that the emperor should do only few things or even nothing so as to give freedom to local areas. This would let the people become rich and wise on the one hand and let local areas develop freely on the other, before ultimately accumulating abundant thoughts and wealth.

If the gentry's power overly expand, of course, or the central government would become less powerful than local areas, then it would be impossible for administrative orders of the central government to work, whereas local squires would become too influential to follow instructions from higher levels. This also would adversely affect political stability. How to balance the emperor's and the gentry's powers, therefore, was a major managerial issue for political organizations in traditional China. The book "*Zizhi Tongjian*" (literally "Comprehensive Mirror to Aid in Government", a pioneering reference work in Chinese historiography) taught emperors the ways of ruling the country, especially worshipping God, following the ancestry, accepting the ministers' opinions, and setting themselves a good example for the people. Although it does talks about underhand tactics, this book is mainly about how to become a leader who need not do anything. Unfortunately, a great many people think of underhand tactics as the most important part of Chinese management. They remind us of the story of the blind men and an elephant.

On the one hand, Chinese intellectuals were supposed to stand for the Confucian orthodoxy before the central government to contain the expansion of the emperor's power. On the other, they were supposed to educate local people so that the existing order could be maintained. In other words, they played the role of an ethical leader who was to establish the value system, set cultural norms, and conduct guanxi management, thereby preventing self-organized units from becoming disorderly. As the local social and political elite, the gentry played an immediate role in resisting intervention of the emperor's power. They could complain, through their connections at higher levels, to the group of high-rank officials in cases where local areas became overburdened because the central government was too greedy for local resources or the hierarchy was adding much to their financial burden. A member of the gentry, if he had served as an official in the capital of the country, could communicated directly with a particular central government official to convey local public opinion. He could rely on a protest by the clerisy and the Confucian orthodoxy to refute the administrative order as departing from local conditions and being arbitrary. Alternatively, he could rely on his own influence to bargain with the county governor so as to protect the local self-organization. Fei Xiaotong referred to the structure with the hierarchical power at the upper level and self-organized units at the lower one as "dual lane political systems."

In China, the rational system is hidden since Confucians advocate management through the natural system. Chinese people always speak highly of ethical behavior such as having brotherly love for others, being cultured and polite, and setting oneself a perfect ethical example to educate the people. In contrast, they generally refer to   bureaucratic civil servants who know nothing but following laws, orders and processes as being mediocre, being good only at paperwork, being ignorant of generally accepted practices, or even being tyrannical and ruthless. But a real intellectual official should play the role to educate general people on the one hand, and resist the emperor's power for them on the other. As a result, managerial thoughts around the natural system are welcome in China, whereas those around the rational system are suppressed. Overcorrection may occur in China – sometimes rituals are valued while laws are not. And this unbalance would sometime cause social disorder.

We may say, therefore, that Chinese managerial philosophies pay more attention to the natural system than to the rational one.

In reality, the traditional Chinese wisdom never denies the importance of the rational hierarchy, not to mention that its principles, such as specialization, impersonalization, institutionalization, documentation and standardization remain good solutions to a great many managerial problems in China. Nonetheless, hierarchy has weaknesses despite its strengths, according to the results of numerous studies. The Chinese always know that there are two sides for everything and place more emphasis on the harmony between Yin and Yang. When employing a certain management system to solve problems, therefore, we must become aware of its negative effects, especially because they will be aggravated by particular characteristics of the Chinese culture. We should not believe, therefore, that this system is a panacea to all managerial problems. Instead, we should think carefully of how to leverage our strengths while minimizing our weaknesses.

Fei Xiaotong noted that the Chinese interacted with each other in differential mode of association, and thus were best at social exchanges. This differs from the type of collectivism in Japan and individualism in Europe and America. Liang Shuming pointed out that the Chinese society was based on family ethics; Francis L. K. Hsu said that the Chinese were situation determinism, as a focal leader always categorize people into inside or outside a particular circle, within an organization, and close allies or general partners, outside it. Management based on the favor-exchange rule generally applies to circle members, whereas the principle of "Business is business" applies to people outside the circle – that is, they are required to follow orders and rules in the hierarchy and the favor-exchange rule does not apply. How big is this circle? How to balance the favor-exchange rule within the circle and the general equity rule? To what extent should people be granted the power to form a self-organized unit? And to what extent should a hierarchy be established to strengthen control? All these depend upon the situation and need to be dynamically balanced.

This is why Yang Guoshu, Hwang, Kwang-Kuo, He Youhui, etc., believe that methodological relationalism should be employed to research Chinese issues, while western management scientists also always regard "guanxi" as a core issue in the research on Chinese management.

There are also numerous western theories that involve social ties, social networks and their management; they are included in the research on social networks. Social exchanges within organizations and differences between being inside and outside circles are also discussed in western managerial theories led by the Leader-Member Exchange Theory (the LMX Theory). But they were put forward more recently and have been less researched since they are less important phenomena in the West. By comparison, favor exchanges constitute a main phenomenon in Chinese organizations, so they are the most important issue that deserves in-depth research by Chinese management scholars.

Why are relationships and social exchanges among the main issues regarding Chinese management? Briefly, the Confucian culture emphasizes the differential mode of association in which people are dealt with in ways depending upon their relationships with a particular person. Accordingly, only people in a small circle who are believed to be "family members" need to follow the interaction principle of pursuing family ethics rather than personal gains. On the other side of the differential mode of association, the social exchange principle of "intercourse for gains" still applies to most people; people in the outer ring of the circle can explicitly mark prices and bargain in exchanges, but those closer to the center of the circle include more family ethics in exchanges. In reality, a great many people who call each other "brother" are also making social exchanges under the banner of "family ethics." Accordingly, Chinese people spend most time and energy making favor exchanges in their organizations or the business world so as to expand their egocentric guanxi network that comprise rings of relationships between them and others. And egocentric guanxi network assures future access to resources, success and safety.

With regard to the foundations of social exchanges in the Chinese society based on family ethics, favor exchange and equal sharing in we-group are required in addition to "mutual benefit." When social exchanges between Chinese people are employed for managerial purposes, a large number of circles can be built in a company, where a good leader will play the leading role on the basis of favors, equity and equal sharing. At the same time, huge networks of outsourcing service providers and of strategic alliances can also be built outside the organization. Likewise, the leader of the core company will organize these peripheral companies by the favor-exchange rule, equity and equal sharing. Good companies of course respect regulations and operational processes, which guarantee the workflow efficient and effective, but flexibility is available beyond institutional arrangements thanks to the Chinese dream of making laws simple. Now that the rules of favor exchange, equity and equal sharing are available, flexible room in workflows will not be abused. On the contrary, good balance between them has become the critical factors for Chinese enterprises' elasticity and responsiveness.

Based on these natures of Chinese society, a good leader put first priority to cultivating oneself, guanxi management, building up egocentric guanxi network, forming guanxi circles, balancing dynamically the favor-exchange rule and equal sharing, and the interests inside and outside circles, so as to create a harmony working environment. He or she also knows how to motivate followers by favor exchanges and enfeoffment, govern the self-organized units under rituals, and balance dynamically the rule of rituals and laws. Bureaucratic principles, hierarchical system, regulations and business processes are certainly important for a good Chinese leader, but these are generally put in the second place for complementing the insufficiency of guanxi management.

Chinese are able to realize elastic production and respond rapidly to customer needs because they have organizations with a network-like structure on the one hand and successful guanxi management on the other. With the resulting elasticity and changeability, Chinese people can hold quick negotiations about everything and make immediate changes. We have developed some very successful management methods, but unfortunately, a great many local management scholars turn a blind eye to managerial phenomena in China, such as guanxi circle, close cliques, operating in the name of another, internal contracting, networks and regional groups of businesses, or even denounce them as being "dregs of feudalism" or "cultural dregs." On the other hand, they have done far from enough to localize valuable western managerial practices, much less develop new theories from local practices.

It is true that relationships are excessively or wrongly used in China such that phenomena including making deals through the back door, abusing privileges, closed cliques and infighting prevail throughout China. Consequently, corruption cases tend to involve groups of people. All these are negative phenomena in a guanxi-oriented society. Like we should not stop eating just because we choked on some food, however, we should think carefully about how to carry out guanxi management so as to leverage our advantages in response and flexibility on one hand, and to minimize weaknesses such as forming closed cliques for private gains and trading in back doors on the other. This relies on efforts made to research Chinese indigenous management.

Chinese ancestors have developed a set of managerial principles in a society based on Confucian family ethics over the past two millennia. We can't help asking: Why does China have such managerial wisdom as part of its traditions? What role can this wisdom play in today's private and public organizations? How can we combine this wisdom with modern managerial practices so as to create modern management theories of China?

Reference

1. Aoki, M. 2001. *Toward a comparative institutional analysis*. MA: MIT press.

2. Barnard, C. I. 1938. *The functions of executive*. MA: Harvard University press.

3. Barnes, J. A. 1954. Class and committees in a Norwegian island parish. *Human Relations*, 7: 39- 58.

4. Blau, P. 1964. *Exchange and power in social life*. NY: Wiley.

5. Bourdieu, P. 1984. *Distinction: A social critique of the judgment of taste (R. Nice, Trans.)*. MA: Harvard University press.

6. Browning, L. D., & Shetler, J. C. 2000. *Sematech: Saving the U.S. semiconductor industry*. TX: A&M University press.

7. Burt, R. 1992. *Structural holes: The social structure of competition*. MA: Harvard University press.

8. Cai, H., & Jia, W. J. 2009. The reverse order in paying off workers by contractors in the Chinese construction industry: For whom is the market risk reduced by "guanxi "? *Society*, 29: 203-223. (In Chinese)

9. Chen, C. H. 1994. *Subcontracting networks and social life*. Taipei: Linkingbooks. (In Chinese)

10. Chen, C. H. 1995. *Financial networks and social life*. Taipei: Linkingbooks. (In Chinese)

11. Chen, C. C., Chen, X. P. & Meindl, J. R. 1998. How can cooperation be fostered? The cultural effects of individualism-collectivism. *Academy of Management Review*, 23: 285–304.

12. Chi, S. C. 1996. The empirical study in roles of leader's confidant. *Management Review*, 15: 37-59.

13. Chua, R. Y. J., Ingram, P., & Morris, M. W. 2008. From the head and the heart: Locating cognition and affect-based trust in managers' professional networks. *Academy of Management Journal*, 51: 436-452.

14. Chua, R. Y., Morris, M. W., & Ingram, P. 2009. Guanxi vs networking: Distinctive configurations of affect- and cognition-based trust in the networks of Chinese vs American managers. *Journal of International Business Studies*, 40: 490-508.

15. Cook, K. S., & Eric, R. W. 2004. Rice, and Alexander Gerbasi, "The emergence of trust networks under uncertainty: The case of transitional economies--Insight from social psychological research." In J. Kornai, B. Rothstein, & S. Rose-Ackerman(Eds.), *Creating social trust in post-socialist transition:* 193-212. NY: Palgrave MacMillan.

16. Cook, K. S. 2004. *Network, norms and trust: The social psychology of social capital.* Keynote speech in Cooley Mead Award.

17. Earley, P. C. 1994. Self or group? Cultural effects of training on self-efficacy and performance. *Administrative Science Quarterly,* 39: 89–117.

18. Farh, J. L., & Cheng, B. S. 2000. Paternalistic leadership in Chinese organizations: A cultural analysis. *Indigenous Psychological Research in Chinese Societies,* 13:127-180. (In Chinese)

19. Fei, H. T. 1992. *From the soil: The foundations of Chinese society.* Berkeley: University of California press.

20. Granovetter, M. S. 1985. Economic action and social structure: The problem of embeddedness. *American Journal of Sociology,* 91: 481- 510.

21. Granovetter, M. S. 1995. The economic sociology of firms and entrepreneurs. In A. Portes (Ed.), *The economic sociology of immigration: Essays in networks, ethnicity and entrepreneurship*: 128-165. NY: Russell Sage Foundation.

22. Granovetter, M. S. 2002. A theoretical agenda for economic sociology. In M. Guillen , R. Collins, P. England & M. Meyer(Eds.), *The new economic sociology: Developments in an emerging field:* 35-59. NY: Russell Sage Foundation.

23. Granovetter, M. S. Forthcoming. *Society and economy.* Undecided publisher.

24. Haken, H. 1983. Synergetics—nonequilibrium phase transitions and self-organization in physics. *Chemistry, And biology.* NY: Springer-Verlag.

25. Hardin, R. 2001. Conceptions and explanations of trust. In K. S. Cook(Ed.), *Trust in society.* NY: Sage Foundation.

26. Ho, D. Y. F. 1993. Relational orientation in Asian social psychology. In K. Uichol & B. Jhon(Eds.), *Indigenous psychologies: Research and experience in cultural context:* 240-259. Newbury Park: Sage Publications.

27. Hofestede, G. 1980. *Culture's consequences.* London: Sage Publications.

28. Hsu, F. L. K. 1963. *Clan, caste and club.* NY: Van Nostrand Reinhold Co.

29. Hsu, F. L. K. 1983. *The study of literate civilizations.* Taipei: Linkingbooks. (In Chinese)

30. Hwang, K. K. 1987. Face and favor: The Chinese power game. *American Journal of Sociology,* 92: 944-974.

31. Hwang, K. K. 1988. *The Chinese power game.* Taipei: Linkingbooks. (In Chinese)

32. Hwang, K. K. 2001. Confucius relationalism: Theoretical construction and methodological considerations. *Education and Social Research,* 2: 1-34. (In Chinese)

33. Leung, K., & Bond, M. H. 1989. On the empirical identification of dimensions for cross-cultural comparisons. *Journal of Cross-Cultural Psychology,* 20: 133-151.

34. Liang, S. M. 1981. *The comparison between Chinese and western culture.* Taipei: Li-Ren Publishing House. (In Chinese)

35. Liang, S. M. 1982. *The manifesto of Chinese culture.* Taipei: Li-Ren Publishing House. (In Chinese).

36. Liang, S. M. 1983. *The comparison between Chinese and western cultures.* Taipei: Li-Ren Publishing House. (In Chinese)

37. Lin, N. 2001. *Social capital: A theory of social structure and action.* NY: Cambridge University press.

38. Lin, N. 2009. *Society, Government and market.* Keynote speech in first international conference of relational sociology, Xi'an.

39. Luo, J. D. 2005. Particularistic trust and general trust: A network analysis in Chinese organizations. *Management and Organizational Review,* 3: 437-458.

40. Luo, J. D. 2011. Guanxi revisited--An exploratory study of familiar ties in a Chinese workplace. *Management and Organizational Review,* 7: 329-351.

41. Mayer, A. C. 1966. The significance of quasi-groups in the study of complex society. In M. Banton (Ed.), *The anthropology of complex societies:* 97-122. NY: Frederick A. Praeger Publishers.

42. Mayo, E. 1945. *The social problems of an industrial civilization.* MA: Harvard University press.

43. McGregor, D. 1960. *The human side of enterprise.* NY: McGraw-Hill.

44. Mishra, A. K. 1996. Organizational responses to crisis: The centrality of trust. In R. M. Kramer & T. R. Tyler (Ed.), *Trust in organizations.* London: Sage Publication Inc.

45. Morris, M. W., & Peng, K. 1994. Culture and cause: American and Chinese attributions for social and physical events. *Journal of Personality and Social Psychology,* 67: 949–971.

46. Oliver, P., Marwell, G., & Teixeira, R. 1985. A theory of the critical mass. I. Interdependence, Group heterogeneity, And the production of collective action. *The American Journal of Sociology,* 91: 522-556.

47. Ostrom, E. 1990. *Governing the commons: The evolution of institutions for collective action.* NY: Cambridge University press.

48. Ostrom, E. 1998. A behavioral approach to the rational choice theory of collective action: Presidential address. *American Political Science Association,* 92: 1- 22.

49. Perrow, C. 1986. *Complex organization: A critical essay.* NY: McGraw-Hill.

50. Powell, W. 1990. Neither market nor hierarchy: Network forms of organization. *Research in Organizational Behavior,* 12: 295-336.

51. Prigogine, I. 1955. *Thermodynamics of irreversible process.* NY: Ryerson press.

52. Scott, W., & Davis, G. F. 2007. *Organizations and organizing—Rational, Natural and open system perspectives.* TX: Pearson Education Inc.

53. Selznick, P. 1943. An approach to a theory of bureaucracy. *American Sociological Review,* 8: 47-54.

54. Shapiro, D. L., Sheppard, B. H., & Cheraskin, L. 1992. Business on a handshake. *Negotiation Journal,* 8: 365-377.

55. Shen, Y. 2007. *Market, class and society: Critical issues on sociology of transformation.* Beijing: Social Science Academic press. (In Chinese).

56. Watts, D. J. & Strogatz, S. H. 1998. Collective dynamics of small-world networks. *Nature,* 393: 440-442.

57. Watts, D. 1999. Dynamics and the small-world phenomenon. *American Journal of Sociology,* 105: 493-527.

58. Williamson, O. 1985. *The economic institutions of capitalism.* NY: The Free press.

59. Williamson, O. 1996. *The mechanisms of governance.* NY: Oxford University press.

60. Yamagishi, T., and Yamagishi, M. 1994. Trust and commitment in the United States and Japan. *Motivation and Emotion,* 18: 129-166.

61. Yamagishi, T., Cook, K. S., & Watabe, M. 1998. Uncertainty, trust, and commitment formation in the United States and Japan. *American Journal of Sociology,* 104: 165-195.

62. Yang, K. S. 1995. Chinese social orientation: An integrative analysis. In T. Y. Lin, W. S. Tseng, & Y. K. Yeh(Eds.), *Chinese societies and mental health:* 19-39. Hong Kong: Oxford University press. (In Chinese).

63. Zhai, X. W. 2001. *The logics of Chinese behaviors.* Beijing: Peking University press. (In Chinese).

64. Zhai, X. W. 2005. *Renqing, Mianzi, Reproduction of power.* Beijing: Peking University press. (In Chinese).

65. Zhang, J. Q., & Luo, J. D. 2007. Network dynamics of clique formation in organization. *Society,* 27:152-164. (In Chinese).

CPSIA information can be obtained at www.ICGtesting.com
Printed in the USA
BVOW02*2105190215

388373BV00006B/20/P